ABA
Tools of the Trade

EASY DATA COLLECTION FOR THE CLASSROOM

SAM BLANCO, PHD, BCBA, LBA
VAL DEMIRI, PHD, BCBA-D, LBA

Copyright © 2017 Different Roads to Learning

Published by

Different Roads to Learning, Inc.
12 West 18th Street, Suite 3E
New York, NY 10011

Telephone: 212 604 9637 Fax: 212 206 9329

www.difflearn.com

All rights reserved. Permission is granted for the user to photocopy limited quantities of the program sheets and data sheets for instructional or administrative use only (not for resale). No other part of the material protected by this copyright notice may be reproduced or used in any form or by any means, electronic or mechanical, including photocopying and recording or by any information storage and retrieval system without prior written permission by the copyright owners.

Printed in the United States

Library of Congress Number: 2017950440

ISBN Number: 978-09907083-7-7

Illustration and Design by Melissa DiPeri Design, LLC.

Many people helped us along the way to getting this book published.

We would both like to thank the teachers, behavior analysts, and speech-language pathologists who provided feedback at different points in the process: Erica Lau, Jennifer Leach, Linda McSorley, Megan Randall, Krishna Ruano, Michael Selbst, Erin Stone, AnneMarie Wallace Hanley, Jim Woodbury, and Elena Zaklis.

TABLE OF CONTENTS

SECTION ONE: INTRODUCTION — 7

    Data Collection — 10

    Tools — 13

SECTION TWO: DATA COLLECTION — 23

    Ten Rules of Data Collection — 25

    Ethics in Data Collection — 26

    A Task Analysis of Data Collection — 28

SECTION THREE: BASICS OF BEHAVIOR CHANGE — 33

    Functional Behavior Assessment — 35

    Antecedent Strategies — 38

    Functional Communication Training — 42

    Addressing Common Issues in Data Collection — 44

    Accessing the Literature — 46

SECTION FOUR: BEHAVIORS — 49

    Common Problem Behaviors — 54

    Adaptive Behaviors — 70

    Pivotal Skills — 71

    Self-Help — 74

    Leisure — 77

    Changing Your Own Behavior — 80

    Classwide Behavior Change — 83

SECTION FIVE: SUPERVISOR MATERIALS — 87

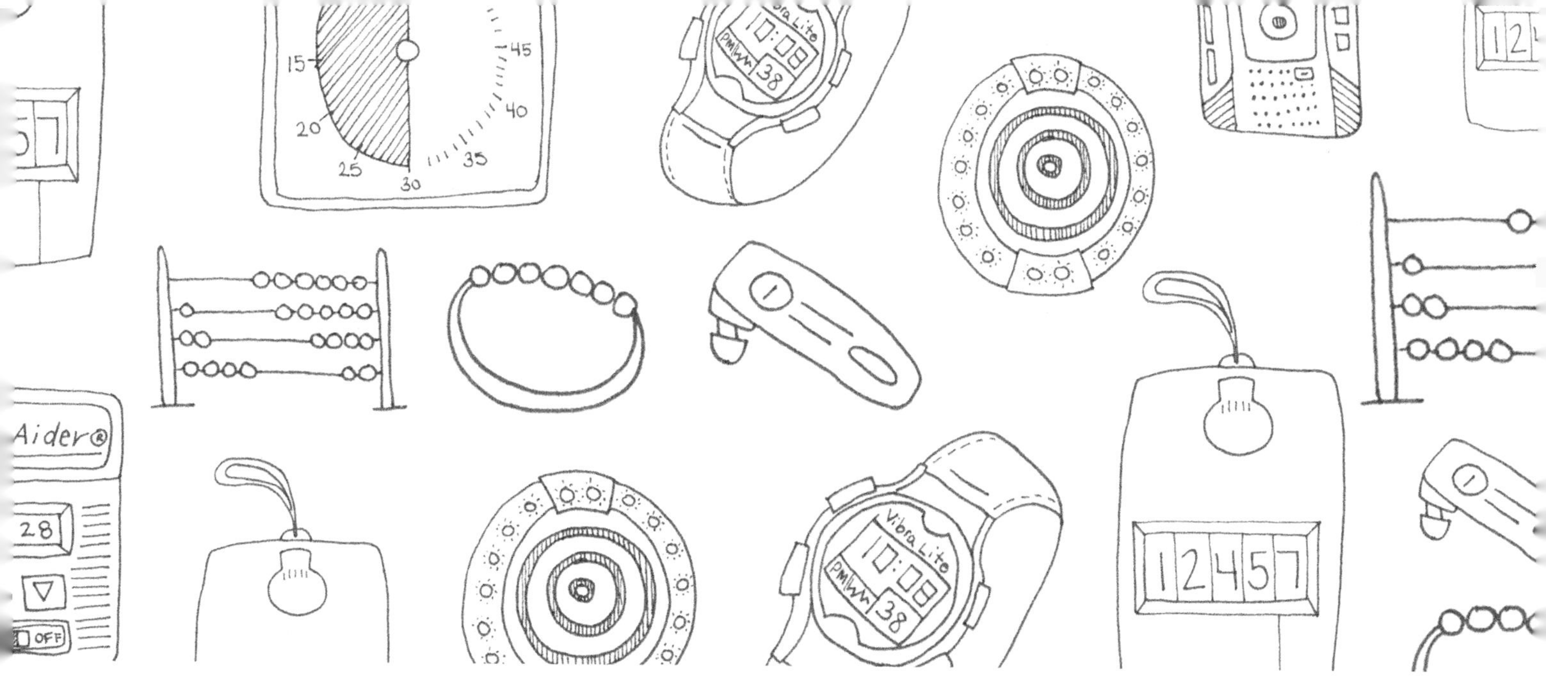

SECTION 1:
Introduction

Who is this book for?

This book is for any teacher or practitioner who works in an environment where data collection is required. This includes new teachers and practitioners who have little practice in data collection, as well as more seasoned teachers and practitioners who are looking for new tools and strategies.

In addition, the book is aimed toward new behavior analysts entering the field, as well as those studying for their Board Certified Behavior Analyst (BCBA), Board Certified Assistant Behavior Analyst (BCaBA), or Registered Behavor Technician (RBT) credentials, or those who are new to the field of applied behavior analysis (ABA).

This book is a collection and summary of tools in our field and how to use them to both track behavior and effect behavior change. It was written to:

- address the need to highlight tools that are available in the field of behavior analysis;
- put practitioners back in touch with the literature that highlights important dimensions of behavior analysis, such as the technological dimension; and
- promote consistency across our field in how we collect data and use it to help change socially significant behavior.

We hope this book serves as a "how to" resource and springboard for using tools, organizing data and information, and effecting behavior change.

Where to Start

First and foremost, there are behaviors that must be addressed immediately due to ethical concerns. For example, if you have a student who is engaging in aggression, self-injury, or bullying, you would need to put a behavior intervention plan in place as soon as possible.

If the behavior is not one that requires immediate attention due to ethical concerns, your first consideration will be your environment. Be sure you've organized your classroom for success (you have materials available, etc.) then select one behavior to target for change. But, how to choose? We suggest there are two possibilities:

1. Select the behavior that will have the biggest impact. Define "biggest impact" in the way that makes sense for your setting (biggest impact on your student, on you, on your entire classroom).
2. Select the behavior that is the easiest to change.

Once you have fit that intervention into your routine, you can begin to take more data on additional behaviors. The goal is to take good data and use it; not to take as much data as humanly possible.

DATA COLLECTION

We've often asked ourselves, "Why on earth do so many teachers seem to hate taking data?" Is it too hard? Do they not understand why they should take it? When to do it? How to use it? Personally, we have been through the rigmarole of the above questions, and our experience tells us that not having the tools available and data sheets ready can serve as a significant barrier to collecting and analyzing data. If you are the only teacher in the class, data collection can seem overwhelming—especially if your class is large and you have several students to attend to. Other barriers to data collection are as simple as not understanding why you are taking the data, or not knowing what to do with it afterward. We have found that if you understand why you take data, you are more likely to do it consistently, especially when you realize that data will directly inform the intervention you use.

If you think about it, humans collect data all the time. For example, we get a physical with our primary care physician annually. What's the data our physician wants to know? All the vitals: blood pressure, heart rate, pulse. Other data routinely taken are weight and height, medications you may take, and exercise routines. If you have diabetes, blood sugar levels…you get the idea! Another example: You engage in exercise. What's your data? Miles run? Stairs climbed? Pounds pressed? Reps completed? One more example (yes, we are driving this point home): you assess and test your students, right? Baseline measures in September, repeated tests throughout the year, comprehensive exams in the spring? This is all data.

Behavior analysts are mostly concerned with measuring behavior that is observable. Now ask yourself what you do with it? Why does your doctor take this data? Perhaps it will inform their interventions, such as being able to prescribe the right medications, recommend the right diet, or order further testing to be done. Basically, doctors need data to give the right intervention and make an informed decision based on the data they have. Why do you track your exercise? Well, if you are training for that marathon you want to be able to run it, so you better know your mileage. Maybe your goal is to lose weight, so you track the calories you've burned and adjust what you are eating. Finally, your students' test scores will inform you on what class to promote them to, what they've learned, what they haven't learned, and where your teaching needs to be focused. Without data, the decisions we make would be biased, incomplete, and may even send us down the wrong intervention path.

Vignette: Shelving the Data

Ms. Leach was considered a highly competent teacher. Her supervisors and colleagues were always impressed with the creative teaching strategies she used with her students and the way she was motivated to individualize programming and really get to know them. She was often the person others went to for data sheets, as she had various forms in her drawers. One day, Ms. Leach's BCBA supervisor asked to review behavioral graphs, and lo and behold, Ms. Leach provided a binder full of data for one particular student. The BCBA was impressed with the details the data sheets included, the specificity of what was written on the data sheets, and the sheer organization of data in a binder. The only thing missing was that nothing had been done with the data. It hadn't been graphed, analyzed, or used in any way. This served as a great supervision goal for Ms. Leach as well as her BCBA.

We often see teachers who do the same thing as Ms. Leach. She faithfully and neatly collected data, but for some reason the process stopped there. Getting to the "use it" part of data seems to be a roadblock for many. We hope to facilitate this, to make it an easy—and maybe even reinforcing—process. Though we understand that graphing might be challenging if you've never done it, it really is something you can learn quickly and do systematically. Once data is graphed, analyzing it is key. You will want to ask, "What is the data telling me? What have I learned from this information about my student's behavior? How can I use this information to change what I am doing so that their behavior improves?" Depending on your role, you will either be assisting with data entry and graphing, or sharing that information with the behavior analyst who will help you analyze the data. You may be in the behavior analyst role yourself.

Choosing a Method for Graphing

In today's tech-savvy world, many of you may already be familiar with computer programs that aid in organizing and understanding data, such as Excel or software applications like Catalyst in which all you do is enter raw data and graphs are automatically generated. For others, the world of technology can be overwhelming, no matter what you are trying to do. When it comes to graphing, simplicity and efficiency is key, and knowing your options for the setting you work in is important. Depending on your goal, you have some options to consider for methods of graphing based on effort, efficiency, and convenience. One common problem is selecting your method for graphing. Below, we outline the pros and cons of each graphing option.

Table 1: Methods for Graphing

Software & Apps for Graphing		Excel		Paper & Pencil	
PROS	CONS	PROS	CONS	PROS	CONS
Templates are already created for you	Crashes	Clean graphs	Learning curve	Fast and efficient	Can get ripped or spilled on; more easily destroyed
Graphs are created for you	May require Wifi	Easier calculations, including trend lines	Each version of Excel is different, have to learn again	Can combine raw data with graphs	More difficult to correct errors
Can share data within a school or district	Limited in scope	Can set up template for data entry and generate simultaneous graphs	Differences on Mac vs. PC	Easier to learn	May look sloppier
	May be costly	Easy to share with supervisor		May have more contact with raw data	May take more time for computation
	May have to pay subscription fees	Very customizable		Very customizable	Need to be prepared with additional graph pages; can't create graphs if you run out
	May not be customizable				

Vignette: There is No One-Size-Fits-All Data Sheet

Recently during a supervision session with Ms. Conrad, she reported that her principal wanted to adopt her data sheets for the entire school. The principal was so impressed with the work being done in the autism classroom that she wanted to use similar data processes in all of the other special education programs. The young teacher, though flattered, was also in a panic because she felt she didn't know if the data sheets she used were beneficial to all special education classrooms in her school. This experience was a great springboard for starting a dialogue about the type of data and systematic process that the principal wanted to set up, as well as learning about her own skills in data collection and how to set up these systems.

A data sheet that works beautifully in one environment may not be appropriate for use in another environment. (For instance, perhaps Ms. Conrad provides reading instruction with her students in dyads, but in another classroom the teacher provides reading instruction in small groups of six. Ms. Conrad's data sheets might not be appropriate for that format of instruction.) Oversimplification of behavior measurement can result, leading to poor and unreliable measures. Finding the right balance is a matter of understanding your learner and the context of the behavior, as well as your skills in observation and behavior measurement (LeBlanc, Raetz, Sellers, & Carr, 2016).

Considerations For the School Setting

- You must consider both the individual and the group simultaneously.
- You may be responsible for training parents, teaching assistants, and/or paraprofessionals on interventions.
- You may be required to complete specific paperwork for your district before creating and implementing interventions.
- You may have set parameters for how data is taken and organized.
- You may have more disruptions, such as fire drills, substitute teachers, or assemblies.
- You may be required to complete specific trainings before addressing some behaviors (such as a crisis intervention training).

Anatomy of a Data Sheet

REQUIRED CONTENT:
- Basic identifying information (i.e., student name, ID of data collector)
- Clearly defined target behavior
- Unit of measurement (based on the dimension of the behavior you are measuring)
- Space to include the date(s) of data collection
- Procedures/instructions on collecting data

OPTIONAL CONTENT:
- Materials required for data collection (attaching items to data sheet or a picture of required items)
- Suggestions for generalization to new objects, people, or environments

CONSIDERATIONS:
- Best size and location for your data sheet:
    - Where will it be optimal for you to record data during sessions/lessons?
    - Is it more beneficial to have something on a clipboard, or something smaller you can slip in your pocket?
    - Will you need a bag to carry your tools, data sheet, timers, pencils, MotivAiders, and phone?
- Is the information organized in such a way that other practitioners can understand it and utilize it?

TOOLS

What are the tools for behavior change? For that matter, what is a tool? It's easy to think about the tools used in other professions: carpenters use hammers and saws, seamstresses use measuring tapes and needles, surgeons use scalpels. But the tools of behavior change are rarely mentioned. A definition of tool is "anything used as a means of accomplishing a task or purpose" (dictionary.com, 2017).

The field of behavior analysis has been concerned with tools from the beginning. In the very first issue of the *Journal of Applied Behavior Analysis* (JABA), there was a "technical note" with information about a wrist counter for recording behavior rates (Lindsley, 1968). In the second issue, there were two "technical notes": one about a five-channel manual counter and another with the schematics for creating your own "miniature, portable time and audible signal-generating device" (Mattos, 1968; Worthy, 1968).

Fortunately for us, it's no longer necessary to create our own devices for measuring and changing behavior. However, it is a challenge to learn about the tools that are available. JABA continued to regularly publish information about such tools throughout the 1970s, but over time these items appeared less and less frequently in its pages. Simultaneously, there have been major shifts in the technology available for teachers to use.

Some journals continue to discuss tools for measuring and changing behavior, including *Teaching Exceptional Children* (a great example is the 2016 article by Margaret Schulze about implementing self-management and how to use tools in doing so), *Tech Trends,* and *Behavior Analysis in Practice.* However, sometimes you may come across a study in which the researchers used a MotivAider to reduce a problem behavior, but you're left wondering, well, how exactly did they do that? Or if you see "abacus" listed as a tool for measuring behavior with no further description, you may have no idea how that would even work.

While these journals and others continue to publish work to educate practitioners, when we first sat down to discuss this book, we quickly realized that in all our years of training, tools for behavior change weren't discussed. One major goal of this book is to help you quickly identify the tools that are available to you and will be the most effective in your situation.

When studying applied behavior analysis or special education, there are chapters devoted to methods of data collection. What is frequently left out, though, are clear explanations of the basic tools that can help you with data collection. A knowledge of the tools at your disposal can only improve your practice.

There are essentially two categories of tools in the field of ABA: tools for measuring behavior and tools for effecting behavior change. Johnston & Pennypacker (1993) defined measurement as "the process of assigning numbers and units to particular features of objects or events" (p. 91).

When selecting a tool, the first thing you'll need to decide is what type of measurement you'll be taking. In other words, what feature or dimension of the behavior will you be measuring? There are several dimensions of behavior that you can measure.

Table 2: Dimensions of Behavior

Dimension	Definition	Examples
Count	Simple tally of the number of occurrences	Susan tallies how many times Aaron raises his hand in math class. "Aaron raised his hand six times in math class."
Rate/Frequency	The number of responses per unit of time	Tom records how many times Demetrius curses per minute, for a ten-minute sample. "Demetrius cursed an average rate of three times per minute."
Duration	The amount of time in which behavior occurs	Leticia measures how long Max lay on the floor, kicking and screaming. "Max lay on the floor, kicking and screaming for 17 minutes."
Latency	The elapsed time between the onset of a stimulus and the initiation of a subsequent response	Marcos measures how long it takes for Jenny to begin writing in her journal after the teacher gave the instructions. "Jenny showed a latency of four minutes before following teacher's instructions to write in her journal."
Inter-response time	The amount of time that elapses between two consecutive instances of a response class	Carson measures the amount of time between each instance of Dylan's tapping on the teacher's shoulder for attention. "Ten seconds passed between Dylan's first initiation and a second initiation for attention."
Intensity/Magnitude	The force with which a response is emitted	Selena measures the intensity of Lisa's self-injury of biting self, based on gradations of marks left on skin. 1 = contact with skin, no marks 2 = teeth marks on skin 3 = broken skin, visibly red/bleeding
Celeration	The change in rate of responding over time	"Johnny requests less than one reinforcer per minute and the teacher is interested in increasing his requests to be at least three per minute in a one week period."

(Note: Definitions are from Cooper, Heron, & Heward, 2007.)

A wide range of both high-tech and low-tech tools are available to help collect data effectively and efficiently. High-tech items include wireless technology or apps, while low-tech may be as simple as a piece of masking tape and a marker. Neither is more valuable than the other, and sometimes combining high-tech and low-tech tools produce the best outcome. For example, you may use a MotivAider to measure intervals and stickers to indicate the occurrence or nonoccurrence of a target behavior within each interval.

When selecting a tool to measure behavior, here are a few questions you should consider:

- Is the tool appropriate for the type of measurement I need? (For example, you would not select a counter if you wanted to measure duration.)
- Is the tool easy for me to use while teaching?
- If the tool is not easy to use while teaching, but is the best tool for the type of measurement I require, how can I modify the environment to increase ease of use?
- Will the tool I'm using cause any distraction or disruption in my classroom? If so, how can I address that?
- Are there any steps needed to ensure the tool is in working order? (For example, if you're using a video recorder, it must be charged prior to each data collection session.)

Without thinking through this process in advance, you may discover that one student's fascination with your audio recorder completely derails your whole lesson, or forgetting to resupply the buttons for your classwide behavior system results in student revolt. Taking a few moments to fully consider these questions, select the best tool for your needs, and troubleshoot any potential implementation problems sets you up for success.

Now let's take a look at the tools. When selecting a tool, first consider the behavior, then the environment, then your own comfort level using the tool in that environment.

Table 3: Overview of Tools

Device	Description	Example
Counter	A counter is one of the most basic tools you can use. Loop a string through the ring, and you can wear it around your neck or hang it in a convenient location. You can also loop it through an apron string and have cards and reinforcers in the pockets. **Strengths:** Easy to use, very portable. **Limitations:** It's a little bit loud, and a little more obtrusive than other data collection tools. It has the potential to become an auditory stimulus.	**Example:** Often used for prompted and unprompted behaviors, more for increasing manding. Any frequency count. Converted to rate per unit of time. Tally how many times a student calls out during class (i.e., the student called out 24 times).
Abacus Counter	This is a simple counter you can create for yourself using beads and a piece of pipe cleaner. It serves the same function as a counter. **Strengths:** It is unobtrusive. You can count behaviors without your students noticing or drawing attention to the counter. **Limitations:** There is a limit to how many beads you can place around your wrist, so consider using an abacus for a very low frequency behavior.	**Example:** Counting a behavior, such as greeting friends during circle time.

Device	Description	Example
 **MotivAider**	The MotivAider is a simple electronic device that vibrates at timed intervals to provide an individual with a private prompt to engage in a specific behavior. **Strengths:** You can use this for tracking many different behaviors, including self-monitoring. You can teach without needing to remember to take the data. **Limitations:** Takes some practice to learn all the settings/programming, cost.	**Example:** Teacher wears it on her belt loop to remind herself to give verbal praise to students or "catch students being good." She sets it for two-minute increments, then delivers verbal praise to students each time she feels it vibrate.
 **VibraLite MINI Watch**	Like the MotivAider, this device vibrates at timed intervals to provide an individual with a private prompt to engage in a specific behavior. **Strengths:** You can use this for tracking many different behaviors, including self-monitoring. Less obtrusive than the MotivAider. **Limitations:** The battery needs to be replaced every few weeks, so that should be considered if the watch will be in use all day for several days. It is also more difficult to program than the MotivAider.	**Example:** A fourth-grade student wears it on his wrist to learn self-monitoring. It is set to vibrate every three minutes. When it vibrates, the student circles a happy face if he has remained "on task" or circles a sad face if he stopped working or talked with a peer during independent work. Once he earns five happy faces, he gets to take a two-minute break doing one of his favorite activities.
Classroom Decibel Meter, such as Too Noisy (App)	This app provides a visual for students based on the decibel level in the classroom. **Strengths:** It's a clear visual reminder for students. It allows students to monitor their own volume rather than relying on teacher prompts. It can be run on a tablet or displayed on a SmartBoard if the tablet is connected to it. It also has a built-in rewards system. **Limitations:** This app is great for the classroom, but is not an actual decibel meter, so you can't see a number associated with the noise level. There are some behavioral goals where you may want to know the actual decibel level.	**Example:** Mrs. Johnson wants to decrease the number of times she has to vocally prompt students to be quiet. She implements a classroom decibel meter that is within view of all students during class. She teaches a mini-lesson about how students should use the meter. After they have learned how to use it, the students monitor themselves and sometimes prompt one another to be quieter, while Mrs. Johnson is free to engage in other teaching tasks.

SECTION 1 · Introduction

Device	Description	Example
Time Timer	This tool provides a visual representation of time as it elapses. **Strengths:** The Time Timer is a great visual prompt for students who struggle with time management or latency in responding. It can easily be used independently by students or in conjunction with other tools. It also comes in many different sizes. **Limitations:** It can only be used in minute increments and for no more than 60 minutes.	**Example:** Ms. Kominos works in a second-grade classroom. She has one student, Andy, who struggles with time management, especially during math. She places the Time Timer on his desk and sets it for 10 minutes, then tells Andy he needs to complete the practice problems before the timer runs out. If Andy appears distracted, Ms. Kominos can simply walk by and point to the Time Timer. When Andy completes the task within the allotted time period, he earns points that can be used in the school store.
Wireless Technology	Wireless technology, such as Bluetooth, is found in many devices. It allows someone to speak into an individual's ear without being in close proximity. **Strengths:** It promotes independence. It offers the opportunity to prompt students without being in direct proximity. Reduces stigma of prompting students with disabilities in public locations. **Limitations:** Some students may not tolerate wearing the device on their ear.	**Example:** A student is ordering a meal at a takeout restaurant and requires a prompt to present his credit card when the cashier asks, "cash or credit?"
Wireless Vibrating Pager, Controlled by Remote	This is similar to the MotivAider, but instead of being programmed with specific increments of time, you can control the vibration from a different location using a remote. **Strengths:** Unobtrusive, flexible. Reduces stigma of prompting students with disabilities in public locations. **Limitations:** Cost.	Example: A teacher is trying to increase the number of peer play initiations a student with autism makes on the playground. She can activate the pager to vibrate when an opportunity for initiation arises. This way the interaction occurs more naturally and the peer has no idea a prompt was even made.

Device	Description	Example
Audio Recording Equipment	There is a range of audio recording equipment available, including voice recording apps for smartphones and tablets, and digital recorders. **Strengths:** Great for measuring verbal goals, such as increasing mands or decreasing stereotypic vocalizations. Especially useful for accurately measuring high rates of behaviors that may be difficult to accurately measure while you are teaching. **Limitations:** It may be difficult to block out time to listen to the recordings and take data. With this form of measurement, it is essential that you block out the time necessary for data recording in a timely manner. If you're unable to do so, select a different form of measurement.	**Example:** Joan teaches in a classroom with six children with autism. She wants to record the frequency of peer mands during playtime. She cannot count them while leading the activity, so she turns on a digital recorder, then listens during one of her preps and records the data. For one student, she plays his recorded mands for a novel person and takes data on the number of mands the person could understand.
Video Recording Equipment	Like audio recording equipment, video recording equipment comes in many forms; it may be as easy as tapping the screen on your tablet. **Strengths:** Great for measuring behaviors that are difficult to measure in the moment and do not leave a permanent product. **Limitations:** Same as audio recording equipment.	**Example:** John and Fred are on the playground and video recording is used to collect data on the number of reciprocal verbal exchanges they have on the swing set.
Camera	Using a digital camera or smartphone to take pictures may be a valuable tool. **Strengths:** Allows you to capture permanent products. **Limitations:** You may not always have the camera handy when you need it. If the student is in view of the lens, you also need permission to take pictures and/or videos from the individual and/or the legal guardian.	**Example:** Taking pictures of damaged materials and/or other environmental destructions, such as number of items thrown or damaged or intensity of damage to objects as it relates to self-injurious behavior.

Device	Description	Example
Classwide Behavior Management Systems, such as Class Dojo	This is a computer-based behavior management system focused on positive reinforcement. It is accessible by both a website and a smartphone app. It is a classwide intervention with multiple layers of application to behavior needs of students. **Strengths:** The primary strength is that it focuses on positive reinforcement and has the potential to change behaviors before they grow in magnitude, intensity, duration, or rate. It also allows teachers to send information and reports to parents. **Limitations:** As with any technology, there is a bit of a learning curve. Class Dojo may not sync with other computer reporting systems the teacher is already required to use.	**Example:** Mrs. Perez wants to increase the behaviors of completing homework on time, being prepared with paper and pencil, and raising your hand to ask a question. She introduces these behaviors to her students and lets them know they can earn points through Class Dojo for doing these three things. Once the class earns a specific number of points, they will get an extra ten minutes of recess.
Data Sheets	For behavior analysts, data sheets are tools created to organize quantitative information on important behavior that is tracked for behavior change. Data sheets specify target behavior definitions, procedures for collecting data and an area to write your information. **Strengths:** Customizable to fit almost any data collection need for individuals and groups. **Limitations:** You need to know the critical information for the behavior/skill you are trying to track. Must know Word/Excel or other software application to create the data sheet if using a computer.	**Example:** Ms. Stone wanted to track each student's response to a greeting during morning circle—specifically if they said, "Good morning, Ms. Stone" in response to Ms. Stone saying good morning to them. She created a group data sheet that incorporated the name of each student and recorded yes or no during morning circle if the student responded correctly when the greeting was presented. The data sheet tracked information for one week.

These are a few common tools that cover many measurement needs of teachers and ABA practitioners. This selection of tools should provide some idea of the types of items available to meet the unique needs of your classroom.

Many tools can be used for both measuring behavior and affecting behavior change. Below we've provided a few examples of the main categories of tools you will be using in the classroom setting.

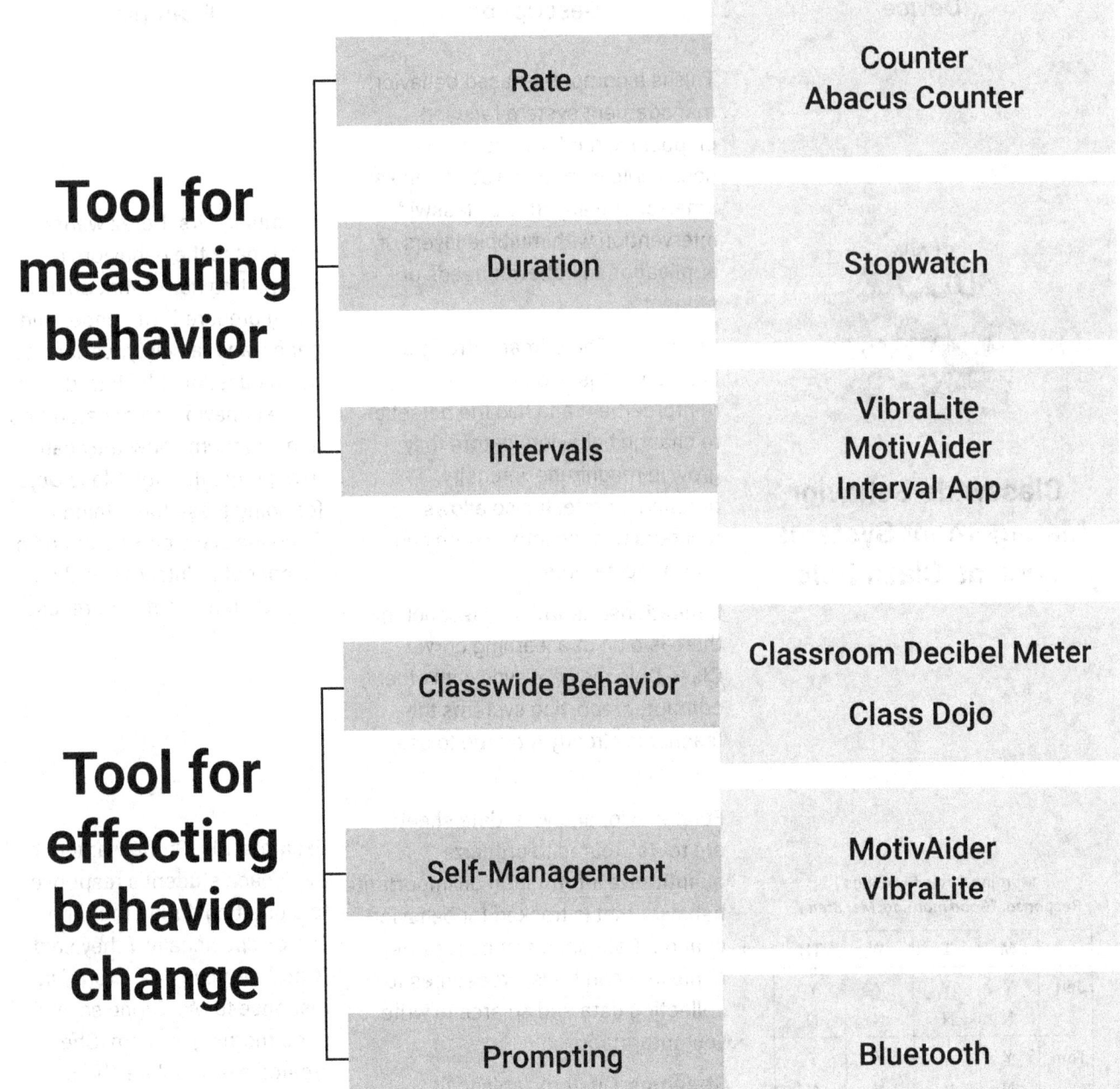

Section One: References and Recommended Readings

Cooper, J. O., Heron, T. E., & Heward, W. L. (2007). *Applied Behavior Analysis*. Pearson: Upper Saddle River, New Jersey.

Johnston, J. M., Pennypacker, H. S., & Green, G. (2010). *Strategies and Tactics of Behavioral Research*. Routledge.

LeBlanc, L. A., Raetz, P. B., Sellers, T. P., & Carr, J. E. (2016). A proposed model for selecting measurement procedures for the assessment and treatment of problem behavior. *Behavior Analysis in Practice, 9*(1), 77-83.

Lindsley, O. R. (1968). A reliable wrist counter for recording behavior rates. *Journal of Applied Behavior Analysis, 1*(1), 77-78.

Mattos, R. L. (1968). A manual counter for recording multiple behaviors. *Journal of Applied Behavior Analysis, 1*(2), 130-130.

Schulze, M. A. (2016). Self-management strategies to support students with ASD. *Teaching Exceptional Children, 48*(5), 225-231.

Dictionary.com, 2017. Retrieved July 10, 2017, from http://www.dictionary.com/browse/tool.

Worthy, R. C. (1968). A miniature, portable timer and audible signal-generating device. *Journal of Applied Behavior Analysis, 1*(2), 159.

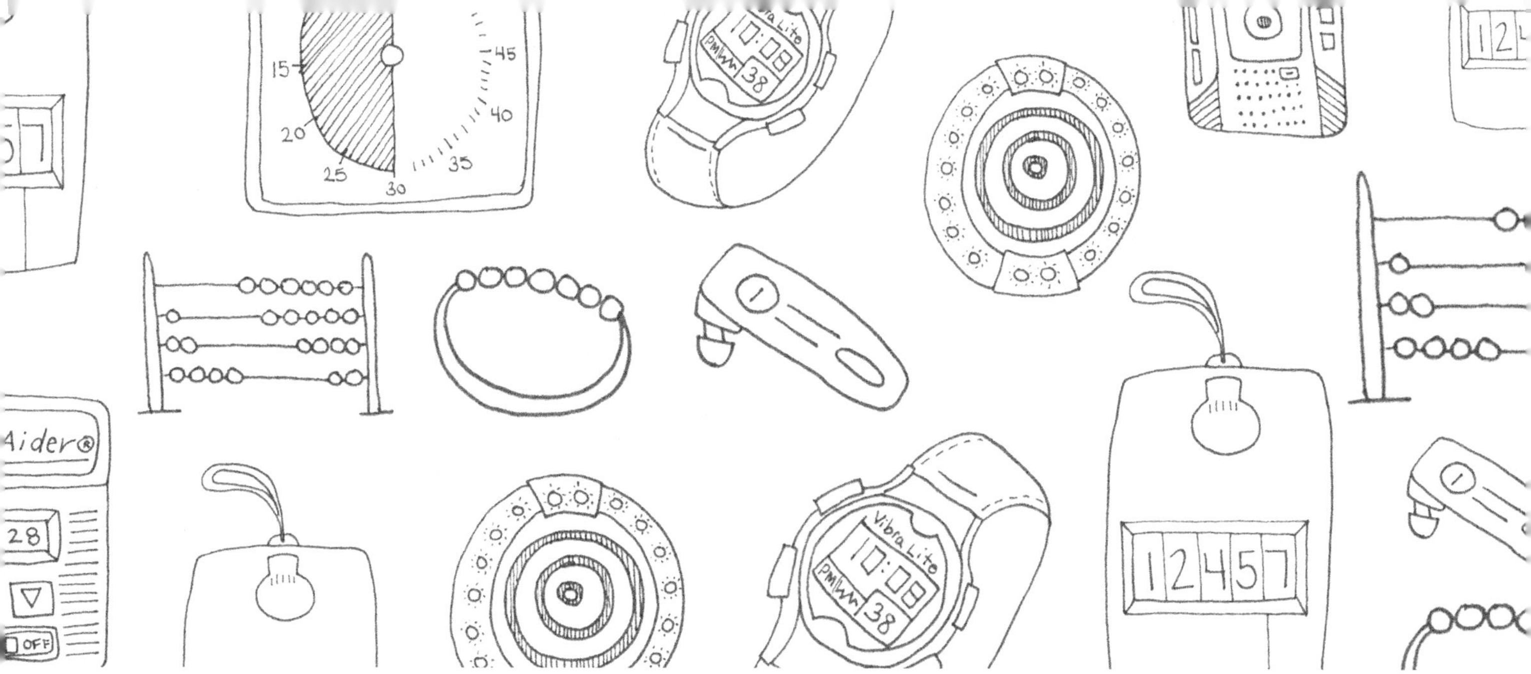

SECTION 2:
Data Collection

Ten Rules of Data Collection

1. **Be ethical.**
   This may seem obvious, but it is probably the most critical rule. Ethical violations occur all the time in data collection. Such violations can range from simple issues (such as marking that a child got a correct response independently when he was actually prompted) to much more severe violations (such as making up data or recording log notes long after the date of the session). Ethical data collection includes clearly defined objectives, explicit parameters for measurement, and consistent, accurate recording of the data.

2. **Do not take data out of fear.**
   The fear of being sued, getting in trouble with the administration, or other legal issues should not be the sole purpose of why you collect data. The goal should always be to collect data you can use to implement interventions or measure progress.

3. **NEVER make up data.**
   Most people don't set out to make up data. But sometimes, people become overwhelmed with the amount of work they have, or may think they remember what happened a half hour ago and add it to their data collection sheet. Memory is notoriously unreliable when it comes to details of day-to-day experiences, so aim to record data as you are working. Go into a session prepared and devote the time to taking the data. You will be glad you did. Finally, sometimes people just forget to take the data and make it up in order to meet demands from a supervisor or administrator. Remember that the data you collect on students is relevant to decisions that impact their lives. You do not want intervention or instructional decisions based on false data.

4. **Take data on observable and measurable behaviors.**
   This is an often overlooked, but very important aspect of data collection. If you do not have a clearly defined, observable, and measurable behavior, then data may be collected differently by different people—or differently by the same person on different days. For instance, if you have a poor definition (such as "tantrum behavior"), when do you begin taking data? Do you take it when the kid yells, or only when his whole body is in contact with the floor? Do you mark the duration of the tantrum, or just count the number of tantrums? Data can get messy very quickly if the behavior is not observable and measurable.

5. **Get permission to take data on an individual's behavior.**
   The child's parent or guardian should be aware of any behaviors targeted for behavior change, *and* should sign a form indicating that they understand and allow the behavior-change procedure and data collection for that procedure. If the child is capable, you should include them in conversations about procedures.

6. **Ensure your intervention is socially valid.**
   Social validity is very important. Ask yourself three questions:
   - *Is this behavior socially significant?* Does the behavior impact the child's life, improve access to academic or social activities, or increase his/her safety? The behavior must be socially significant for the child, not for the teacher or other students.
   - *Are the procedures appropriate?* If the procedures are aversive, are they the best procedures for the desired behavior change?
   - *What is the social importance of the results?* If you ask the child's guardian, do they agree that the results are socially important for the child?

7. **Be objective.**
   Objectivity is at the heart of science, and effective behavior interventions rest on observable and measureable phenomena. Staying objective when faced with desires to see your student do well may be challenging, but remember the saying, "The data doesn't lie." As mentioned before, you must start with an objective definition of the behavior. Subjectivity or other pressures that may be well-meaning can mar real progress and prevent goal achievement. Put your feelings aside and mark only what is observed.

8. **Graph your data consistently.**
   As with recording data, it is highly recommended that data is graphed regularly so that you can visually analyze it to make decisions. What determines a "regular" schedule of graphing will vary, depending on the frequency of data collection based on the behaviors you are measuring. Intensive skill acquisition programs involving language may require more frequent data collection and daily or session-to-session graphing so that decisions can be made. Skills that are targeted less intensively will naturally have less data and therefore less graphing. Never put yourself in a position where you have weeks of data to graph, especially when problem behaviors are being monitored.

9. **Be responsive to your data.**
   Being responsive to your data includes looking at it daily to assess trends: looking at patterns in behavior change and determining whether or not interventions are working. Next, analyze this information to make informed decisions about the procedures you are using with the student. For instance, if you see that a behavior change procedure you implemented three weeks ago is showing an increase in an undesirable behavior, responding to the data would include changing that procedure to increase appropriate behavior.

10. **Use data to make decisions about training staff and yourself.**
    Data can highlight areas of need, both for staff and for yourself. Perhaps you discover that many of your students are struggling with the same behavior problem. This may indicate a need for training to address that particular type of issue. Or maybe you discover through analyzing the data regularly that two colleagues are recording their data in different ways. This would be a sign that you should train staff on the appropriate data collection method.

Ethics in Data Collection

There are many ethical issues to consider related to data collection, including:

Consent from the individual and/or legal guardians

- The requirements for consent are not always the same. For instance, if your learner is at a school in which data collection is part of the overall program, individual consent may not be required for general interventions you put in place. But if you had to conduct a functional behavior assessment (FBA), consent would be required.

- Laws can vary from state to state, and policies related to state laws can vary from city to city, and district to district. It is important to be aware of the laws that impact your particular setting. One excellent resource in understanding federal law is wrightslaw.com. Here you can find information pertaining to educational law, the Individuals with Disabilities Education Act (IDEA), and recent legal cases that may impact your practices.

- While in many situations you may only need the consent of the legal guardian, in some cases you may be required to attain consent from the individual whose behavior is being targeted for change.

Social validity

- When selecting target behaviors, it is essential to consider social validity. This means the "target behaviors are appropriate, intervention procedures are acceptable, and important and significant changes in target and collateral behaviors are produced" (Cooper, Heron, & Heward, 2007, p. 704). There are times when a behavior is targeted actually for the benefit of the teacher, the parent, or the classroom as a whole. It's important that the target behavior be socially valid *for the individual whose behavior is being targeted for change*. In the classroom setting, often this includes that the intervention is acceptable to the parent or guardian.

- Social validity can be determined through the use of a Likert scale, such as the Treatment Acceptability Rating Form - Revised (Reimers and Wacker, 1988). This scale asks questions such as "How acceptable do you find the strategies to be regarding your concerns about the identified learner?" and "How much do you like the proposed procedures?"

Storing data and maintaining confidentiality

- Your school district or organization should have a policy for storing data safely and maintaining confidentiality of students/clients. Often, personal information about students (names, birthdates, social security numbers, etc.) are required to be in a locked cabinet in a locked office.

- Information about your students' behaviors, responses from parents, and interventions should be kept confidential.

Treatment integrity

- This is where it's very important to communicate concisely both the target behavior and the intervention. There are several instances in which it is reported that an intervention is not working, when in actuality the practitioners implementing the intervention have unintentionally strayed from the original plan.
- There are a few things you can do to address this problem:
    - Treatment integrity checks
    - Modeling and practice
    - Clearly defined treatments

Right to effective treatment

- According to the Professional and Ethical Compliance Code for Behavior Analysts, "Clients have a right to effective treatment (i.e., based on the research literature and adapted to the individual client). Behavior analysts always have the obligation to advocate for and educate the client about scientifically supported, most effective treatment procedures. Effective treatment procedures have been validated as having both long-term and short-term benefits to clients and society" (BACB, 2014).
- While you may not be a behavior analyst, it seems only appropriate that any students or clients you work with have the right to effective treatment. You can guarantee this by utilizing evidence-based practices and taking data to demonstrate whether or not the individual is responding to the intervention.

Documenting work for use by future practitioners

- If you're the only teacher or practitioner working with a particular student, it is sometimes easy to become less consistent and descriptive with your data. However, ethically, it is imperative that you document your work well so that future practitioners can use it. It's not uncommon for practitioners to move, leave cases unexpectedly, or reduce their hours due to other commitments. In these instances, strong documentation of your work eases the transition from one provider to the next, gives ample information about the progress of the student and interventions that have worked or not worked in the past, and helps the new provider gain a more complete picture of the student.

State and local laws related to data collection

- It's important to be aware of the state and local laws relevant to data collection in your setting. For instance, there may be particular requirements about how and where data is stored, or who is allowed to see data for a particular individual. You must be in compliance with these laws.

IOA data and drift for behavior being measured

- Interobserver agreement (IOA) data collection is often a significant challenge to any teacher or behavior analyst when it comes to time constraints. However, without IOA data on behaviors being measured, you run the risk of inaccurate data and observer drift. Observer drift simply means that an observer may begin to question and/or change how they are applying the definitions of the target behaviors when they are being measured, which may happen over time.
- To ensure that everyone is measuring the same behavior, the practice of IOA becomes critically important. Planning a time to implement IOA with data collectors is key to preventing such issues and should occur regularly in each phase of intervention and/or data collection. Perhaps most importantly, it is good practice to obtain IOA when you first train a new person to collect data to confirm you are both recording data on target behaviors reliably.

Measuring treatment integrity

- This always comes back to having a clear, concise, and objective intervention. Treatment integrity basically means that you maintain the intervention as it was originally designed. This may result in the teacher or administration believing an intervention didn't work, when they actually can't be sure because the intervention was not implemented consistently.

Sharing raw data

- Some school districts don't allow sharing of raw data, especially with individuals who are not trained to work with data. This is important because out of context, data is at risk for being misinterpreted, manipulated, and/or misused. Always consider the source of who may be requesting raw data and the reasons why; and check with your center, agency, and other organizational bodies on policies related to the sharing of raw data.

A TASK ANALYSIS OF DATA COLLECTION

On the following pages, we have task analyzed the three phases of data collection and the steps to follow to define your behavior/responses and set up your data collection sheets.

Pre-Data Collection Phase

The pre-data collection phase usually involves some kind of referral or identification of an issue by those who work with the student, in which they may express concerns regarding problem behavior in the classroom setting. Often, teachers may contact case managers or other professionals within their school to seek assistance. Depending on the systems and processes in place at your school, you may have to fill out referral forms for a behavior analyst, behavior specialist, psychologist, or other professional responsible for helping you with the problem behaviors of your learners.

Additionally, behaviors that may be qualified as mild to moderate in severity may also have been responded to with various strategies, accommodations, and/or modifications that any good teacher should implement. Important to note in this early phase is that the information collected so far may consist of anecdotal information, based on informal observations or interactions with the student by you or others.

Two big tasks are necessary during the pre-data collection phase: 1) creating a data collection sheet that accounts for what you want to see measured, and 2) figuring out what tools you can use to efficiently track behavior. Though this may take a little bit of time, when done accurately it will save a lot of time later, help you analyze data reliably, and most importantly, help you monitor behavior changes during intervention. This will allow you to then make any necessary tweaks to your intervention strategies. Once you create a formalized data collection system, you will be in a strong position to make informed decisions about interventions for your student. It is important that general behavioral strategies and evidence-based practices are tried first with students before more restrictive measures are taken to intervene. This involves a functional behavior assessment. That being said, the following should occur:

Step 1: **Talk to other professionals and parents about their concerns regarding the learner.** Gather information on what has already been tried for interventions, and types of reinforcement that have been used. How long have such interventions been tried?
- Does the behavior occur at home?
- Does the behavior occur in other places in the community?
- Does the behavior occur in other contexts or is it limited to school?
- Do the parents share your concern?
- Under what conditions and contexts does the behavior occur, as reported by caregivers?
- Has direct positive reinforcement been tried?
- Have clear directives and school rules been stated and identified for the student?
- Have expectations been reviewed for the student?
- Have you reflected on your own behavior(s)? That is, could it be that you may be inadvertently reinforcing behaviors with attention, or escape/avoidance? If so, how and what can you change about your responding?

Step 2: **Operationally define your behavior and put the definition(s) on your data sheet.** Make sure that you and your team are in agreement with the definition of your behavior(s). Ensure that your definition has measureable properties of behavior (e.g., repeatability, temporal extent, and temporal locus) as well as topography and magnitude if needed.

Step 3: **Create your data sheet.**
This is a step that requires some active thinking in terms of how often you are aiming to measure behavior, the actual characteristics of behaviors you are measuring (frequency, duration, etc.), and the

simple instructions required for data collection, as well as the definition. For example, if you know that data collection needs to occur every day, you automatically know you will have rows and/or columns or space to record the behavior every day. Knowing the schedule and when to collect data is key in setting up your data sheet.

Step 4: Select appropriate tools for intervention and measurement.

Think of this step as being part of a kit: the tools or materials for recording the information you need. Often, this involves a clipboard, paper and pencil, and tools such as timers, counters, MotivAiders, or others that you will use during actual data collection.

Data Collection Phase

During this phase, you are most concerned with obtaining baseline (if possible) and tracking the behavior you are interested in with formal data collection methods. If behavior is severe in the form of aggression, self-injury, or has the potential for anyone getting hurt, then an immediate intervention is warranted and baseline data cannot be taken—rather, you just begin data collection in the intervention phase. Once you have written the most accurate, measurable, and comprehensive definition of the behavior to be tracked, you are ready to trial your data collection system. Of great importance is that the individuals assigned to collect the data are trained reliably, and are able to accurately document the behavior or response of concern. To know this, you first have to trial the data collection system yourself. Once you have done this and tweaked any aspects of data collection, you are ready to train others, as well as take data on interobserver agreement (IOA). Finally, what is the schedule of data collection that you should follow (e.g., daily, weekly, monthly, per occurrence of the behavior)? For how long (e.g., ten minutes, a class session, the entire school day)?

Step 1: Trial the data collection system.

Make any necessary changes in recording procedures or tool selections.

Step 2: Decide who will be trained to collect data and train them on the actual behaviors to be observed and measured.

This involves knowing what the behavior looks like and knowing where and how to write it down on the data sheet.

Step 3: Train all parties involved in data collection on how to use the *tools* for collecting data.

For example, when using a MotivAider, does everyone know how to set the interval, respond to the vibration, reset it if needed, change a battery, etc.

Step 4: Conduct interobserver agreement (IOA) on the data collection process.

IOA also helps to guard against "observer drift," a phenomenon in which observers begin to "drift" in how they use the definitions of behavior over time (Cooper, Heron, Heward, 2007). It's a good idea to conduct IOA immediately after the initial data collection training and repeat this process for up to 20%–30% of sessions of data collection, especially if there are any changes to data collection procedures. To translate, if you collected ten sessions of data, three of those sessions would include IOA data. Changes warranting IOA include:

- New people who have to take data on behaviors.
- New phases/changes to intervention procedures.

Step 5: Clearly identify the data collection schedule.

All of this information can and should be included on the data sheet or a procedures sheet clarifying how to collect the data:

- How long data is collected for each session: ten minutes, one hour, the entire school day?
- When data is collected: as soon as the behavior is observed, ten seconds after behavior?
- Where the data is collected? (Note that "where" may need to be clarified for both the data sheet and physical location of the environment, such as the lunchroom, playground, classroom, or gym?)

Post-Data Collection Phase

The Post-Data Collection Phase is an important one—so perhaps the term "post" is not the best to use, as it implies you are done with data collection. Here, we are referring to what should happen when you complete a data collection period. That is, what do you do with the data you have collected for that session, day, or week?

Step 1: **Review your data sheet, noting tallies, marks, comments, timings, etc.**
If there are any questions regarding what is on the data sheet, follow up with the person who recorded the data and get clarification.

Step 2: **Tally, sum, or convert any information into the actual number you will enter on your graph.**
For example, if you tallied how many times your student threw a pencil during the school day, you need to add up all of the pencil throws (e.g., 3, 2, 5, 1, 0, 10 = 21) for that school day. The total number of pencil throws is the final number you are interested in for that day.

Step 3: **Enter your raw data to be graphed onto a computer or actual paper and pencil; construct your graphs.**
- Are your graphs accurately labeled?

Step 4: **Analyze your data.**
- What are the trends?
- What are the levels?
- What is the variability?

Step 5: **Make a data-based decision.**
- Do you have enough data points to be able to make a decision yet?
- Is there anything you can change about your intervention based on the visual inspection of the data?

Step 6: **Set up your clean data sheets for the next day or data collection period and repeat steps 1-6.**

Summary

It is important to plan for each phase in data collection. Effective planning helps you collect better data and optimize your time.

LeBlanc, Raetz, Sellers, & Carr (2016) offered a decision-making model for determining measurement procedures for problem behavior, one that would best measure a target behavior, given the therapeutic and environmental constraints in one's workplace. This decision-making model helps the behavior analyst systematically work down a list of questions to ask regarding the type of target behavior observed. It also considers which resources one has available to determine the best data collection method for a particular behavior, based on important dimensions of that behavior. LeBlanc, et al. (2016) offer an important and practical solution for how to work through real work-setting barriers to make the best possible decision for data collection.

Section Two: References and Recommended Readings

Behavior Analyst Certification Board (2014). Professional and ethical compliance code for behavior analysts. Retrieved April 7, 2016.

Cooper, J. O., Heron, T. E., & Heward, W. L. (2007). *Applied Behavior Analysis*. Pearson: Upper Saddle River, New Jersey.

LeBlanc, L. A., Raetz, P. B., Sellers, T. P., & Carr, J. E. (2016). A proposed model for selecting measurement procedures for the assessment and treatment of problem behavior. *Behavior Analysis in Practice, 9*(1), 77-83.

Reimers, T. M., & Wacker, D. P. (1988). Parents' ratings of the acceptability of behavioral treatment recommendations made in an outpatient clinic: A preliminary analysis of the influence of treatment effectiveness. *Behavioral Disorders, 14*(1), 7-15.

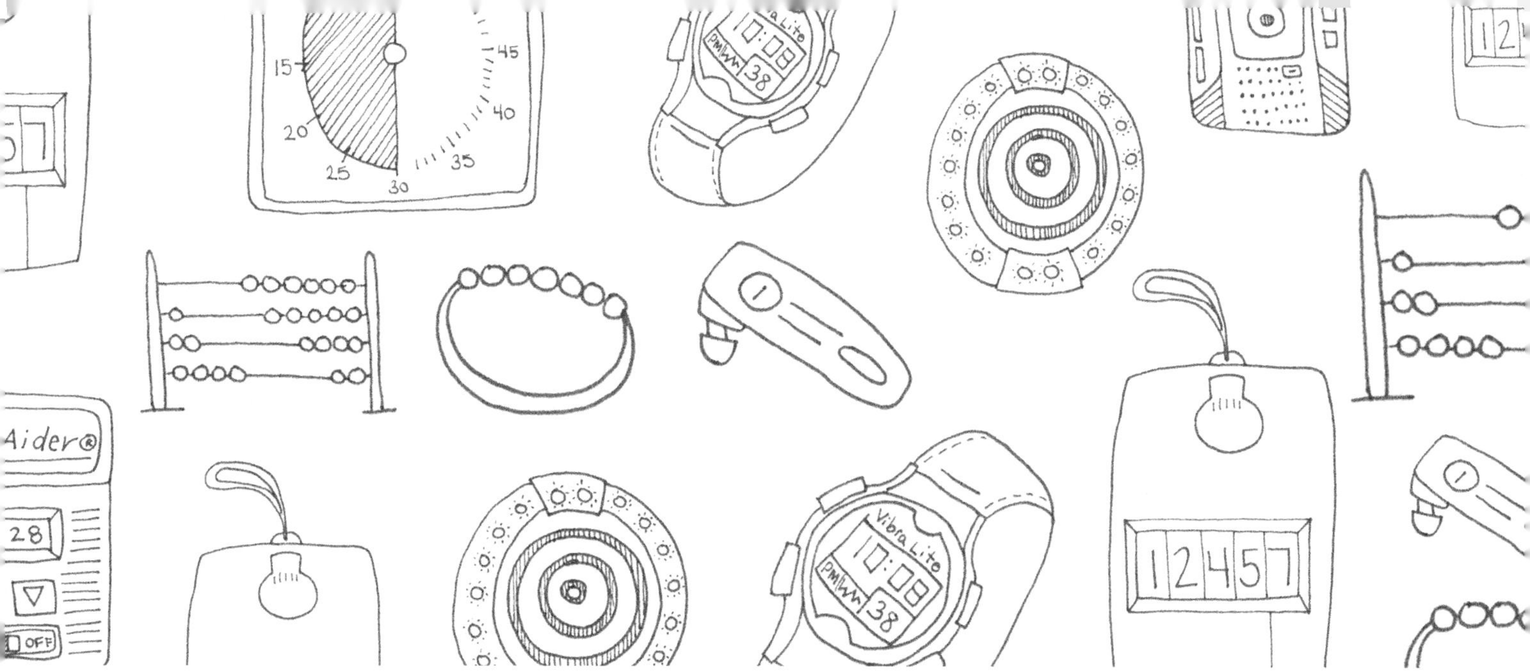

SECTION 3:
Basics of Behavior Change

Functional Behavior Assessment

A Few Words about Functional Behavior Assessments and Behavior Intervention Plans

Although it should go without saying that any behavior intervention plan (BIP) should be based upon a thorough functional behavior assessment of the target behaviors in question, we cannot overstate the importance of this process and assessment. Without a solid understanding of the conditions, variables, and stimuli that contribute to problem behavior, you run the risk of:

- creating a plan that might not be functional;
- guessing as to what interventions might work;
- wasting time on the wrong interventions;
- putting students and staff at risk of further problem behavior, and therefore harm; or
- getting into legal trouble for not conducting an FBA to develop your BIP.

Although many state laws may be unclear regarding who can or cannot conduct an FBA, best practices indicate that professionals who have training and experience conducting FBAs are best for the job. This essentially should point to the need for an experienced Board Certified Behavior Analyst's (BCBA) services. The reauthorization of the Individuals with Disabilities Education Act (IDEA, 2004) delineates the need to engage in prevention-focused interventions rather than traditional disciplinary actions, such as suspensions or expulsions from school. Therefore, at a minimum, an FBA should be conducted when faced with problem behavior that may interfere with the safety of the individual and/or others, or may prevent learning of the individual and/or others (O'Neill, Horner, Albin, Sprague, Storey, & Newton, 1997; IDEA, 2004).

Functional Assessment and Analysis of behavior is one of the most studied technologies of behavior analysis (Hanley, 2012), and has a plethora of evidence to support its use (Hanley, Iwata, & McCord, 2003). Important to understand is that an FBA is a process that has historically involved several hierarchical levels and procedures of: 1) indirect measures, 2) direct measures, and 3) functional analysis (Hanley, 2012).

Functional analysis (FA) procedures for evaluating problem behaviors (Iwata, Dorsey, Slifer, Bauman, & Richman, 1982/1994) are perhaps the most significant in terms of the skill requirement of the professional conducting the analysis, and have the most potential for yielding valuable results for treatment interventions. The expertise of a BCBA is necessary in setting up environmental conditions to systematically manipulate the environmental events suspected of evoking the target behaviors, as other professionals are unlikely to have such specialized training.

See Table 4 (next page) for a description of the FBA types. Knowing how to monitor behaviors, and taking precautions to minimize harm to individuals during an FA, are critical to understand. The entire process of the FBA should result in a confident hypothesis about challenging behavior, the conditions or actions that predict the behavior, the consequences that maintain the behavior, and how the behavior may vary across time. If you are a new BCBA and have never conducted an FBA, you will want to ensure that you work under the tutelage of someone more experienced until you develop that skill yourself—especially for an FA of a potentially dangerous behavior.

Table 4: Types of Functional Behavior Assessments

Types of Functional Behavior Assessments	Tools Used	Weaknesses	Strengths
Indirect Measures	Involve rating scales, questionnaires, and interviews	• No direct observation of the behavior itself • Inherent biases in rating scales • Not as reliable as other types of behavior assessments	• Interview with significant others yields valuable information on when, where, with whom, and with what behavior(s) may occur
Direct Measures Descriptive Assessment	Direct observations of behavior using data collection sheets (such as an ABC data sheet)	• No manipulation of consequential variables purported to affect the target behavior	• Identify form and magnitude of behavior • Helpful in constructing definitions and generating basic hypotheses of functions • Possible antecedent manipulations
Functional Analysis (FA) (including analogue FA, synthesized FA, latency-based FA, trial-based FA, etc.)	Direct observation of behavior using data collection sheets, timers, counters, MotivAiders, and other tools for collecting data	• Requires specialized training in setting up conditions to evoke problem behaviors, and responding to behaviors with reinforcement • May take a great deal of time to complete • May not capture low-rate behaviors • Costly in terms of financial and staffing resources	• Direct observation of target behavior • Systematic manipulation of environmental conditions such as antecedents and consequences of the target behavior • Establishes functions of behavior needed for identifying functional treatments

Efficient Data Collection During the FBA Process

Given the importance we place on understanding functions of behavior, we like to think of data collection during the FBA process the way you'd think of having to bake a fancy cake. It will require prepping, gathering, and accurately measuring the ingredients needed; sequencing and mixing the ingredients in a particular order; then possibly waiting for certain amounts of time for a filling to chill or egg whites to form peaks. You get the idea: the wrong combination of ingredients, not following a sequence of steps, or rushing to bake your pastry can lead to a less than wonderful fancy cake—all because of poor preparation, lack of understanding about why certain sequences have to be followed, or poor measurement.

As with the fancy cake, data collection for the FBA process needs to be precise, efficient, and planned out. You may start with general ideas of what needs to be measured and when, then observe the behavior once, and then hone in on the specifics after you've developed your data sheets and gathered your tools. If you are specifically conducting a functional analysis (FA) as part of your FBA, then the procedures are probably the most involved—in terms of the arrangement of conditions and precise need for data collection—because they will inform everything about treatment based on the function(s) of behavior you obtain. Having the skills to help you quickly identify functions, and then develop treatments based on those functions while monitoring changes in behavior, are quintessential behavior analytic skills. No one is born with these skills, in the same way that a pastry chef is not born knowing how to mix ingredients to produce a wonderful pastry. The collective execution of the above skills will save time, resources, and energy while providing humane and ethical treatment to individuals who need it.

Behavior Intervention Plans and Data Collection

In some ways, the data collection systems for your behavior intervention plan will probably be easiest if compared to the initial FBA you've conducted. This is because the data systems should essentially already be developed, if not identical, to the ones you used to measure baseline target behaviors during your FBA process. Data sheets that you may have used during the FBA process, but will not need for your intervention, may include:

- ABC data sheets, and/or
- descriptive and narrative data sheets.

Everything else you have used to measure target behaviors should be the same. If it's not, you will need to understand why that is the case. For example, as you formulate your interventions, you may create other data sheets to monitor implementation of a point system or self-monitoring system that serves as feedback to the individual. These particular data sheets, though important, are not the actual data sheets measuring the target behaviors you will be graphing.

Functional Assessment: References and Recommended Readings

Bloom, S. E., Iwata, B. A., Fritz, J. N., Roscoe, E. M., & Carreau, A. B. (2011). Classroom application of a trial-based functional analysis. *Journal of Applied Behavior Analysis, 44*(1), 19-31.

Hanley, G. P. (2012). Functional assessment of problem behavior: Dispelling myths, overcoming implementation obstacles, and developing new lore. *Behavior Analysis in Practice, 5*(1), 54-72.

Hanley, G. P., Iwata, B. A., & McCord, B. E. (2003). Functional analysis of problem behavior: A review. *Journal of Applied Behavior Analysis, 36*(2), 147-185.

Individuals with Disabilities Education Act of 2004, P.L. 93-112, 20 U.S.C. para 1400 *et seq.*

Iwata, B. A., Dorsey, M. F., Slifer, K. J., Bauman, K. E., & Richman, G. S. (1982/1994). Toward a functional analysis of self-injury. *Journal of Applied Behavior Analysis, 27*, 197-209. (Reprinted from *Analysis and Intervention in Developmental Disabilities, 2,*3-20, 1982.)

Minshawi, N. R., Hurwitz, S., Fodstad, J. C., Beibl, S., Morriss, D. H., & McDougle, C. J. (2014). The association between self-injurious behaviors and autism spectrum disorders. *Psychology Research and Behavior Management, 7*, 125-136.

O'Neill, R. E., Horner, R. H., Ablin, R. W., Sprague, J. R., Storey, K., & Newton J. S. (1997). *Functional Assessment and Program Development for Problem Behavior: A Practical Handbook* (2nd ed.). Pacific Grove, CA: Brooks/Cole.

Pelios, L., Morren, J., Tesch, D., & Axelrod, S. (1999). The impact of functional analysis methodology on treatment choice for self-injurious and aggressive behavior. *Journal of Applied Behavior Analysis, 32*(2), 185-195.

ANTECEDENT STRATEGIES

Sometimes, in trying to provide appropriate consequences for a behavior, we forget to consider *antecedent strategies*. An antecedent strategy is preventative, and is put in place before the individual has an opportunity to engage in the behavior. Just like any other attempt to create behavior change, basing the antecedent strategy on the *function* of the behavior increases the likelihood that the strategy will be effective. Below are a few examples of types of antecedent strategies you may want to consider implementing.

Focusing on the Positive

In your training to become a teacher, you probably heard the phrase "catch them being good." As a teacher, you want your classroom to be a place students want to be. You should plan in advance to provide students with lots and lots of opportunities to evoke reinforcement. This means that they will receive attention for appropriate behaviors, be allowed to escape difficult tasks by asking for breaks appropriately, and gain access to tangibles (such as games or special pencils) through exhibiting appropriate behaviors.

It can be all too easy to make the classroom a highly punishing environment in which any small infraction results in a verbal reprimand or some other type of aversive consequence. When you're getting ready for the day, it may be helpful to list specific behaviors you want to see your students exhibiting so you can recognize them when they occur. You can read more about this on page 73 (also see the section on Classwide Contingencies, page 74, and Changing Your Own Behavior, page 73).

Changing the Physical Environment

This type of strategy is quite common. For instance, when two children are talking to each other during class all the time, the teacher may change the seating chart and move their desks apart from each other. Other common examples include parents covering outlets before their baby starts to crawl, or a store putting up a "Wet Floor" sign after mopping. Consider also the child who is heavily distracted by stimuli on a wall. Simply removing pictures or stimuli that are distracting may help focus attention to where it is needed.

Changing the physical environment can be very helpful in addressing some problem behaviors, especially when combined with reinforcement strategies (Guardino & Fullerton, 2010). Research has demonstrated that an open environment can improve safety and learning activities in a day-care setting (Twardosz, Cataldo, & Risley, 1974).

Addressing Transitions

When students have to physically transition, it is important to make expectations clear. This may come in the form of visual schedules that are individualized, advance notice of schedule changes, predictability in schedules, and efficient transitions when physically navigating school. Additionally, research has shown that visual schedules alone may not prevent problem behavior. Rather, combining reinforcement and extinction procedures will impact behavior more significantly (Dettmer, Simpson, Myles, & Ganz, 2000; Cote, Thompson, & McKerchar, 2005; Wilder, Chen, Atwell, Pritchard, & Weinstein, 2006; Waters, Lerman, Alyson, & Hovanetz, 2009). When transitioning, consider where the the student is moving from—is it a highly preferred context to a less preferred context, more structure to less structure, high reinforcement opportunities to less reinforcement opportunities—and whether there is consistency of intervention implementations across people and environments.

Noncontingent Reinforcement

This strategy may at first seem counterintuitive, but there is a lot of research demonstrating that providing *noncontingent reinforcement* can be quite effective in changing behavior. Noncontingent reinforcement is simply providing a reinforcer "for free," meaning the individual has access to the reinforcer regardless of their behavior. For instance, let's say that a child frequently interrupts the teacher during instruction after recess. A functional assessment determines that the function of interrupting is social attention from the teacher. The teacher implements an intervention that includes two minutes of one-on-one time with the teacher at the end of recess, before the math lesson begins. Because the child received attention that was noncontingent on her behavior, her problem behavior that functioned for attention decreases during the math lesson.

Noncontingent reinforcement has been used to increase the wearing of hearing aids and orthotics (Richling, Rapp, Carroll, Smith, Nystedt, & Siewert, 2011), decrease self-injurious behavior (Wilder, Normand, & Atwell, 2005), decrease stereotypy (Enloe & Rapp, 2014), and decrease destructive behavior (Hanley, Piazza, & Fisher, 1997), among other things.

Again, it is important to note that a functional assessment and a preference assessment should be completed before implementing a noncontingent reinforcement procedure in order to identify potential functionally-equivalent reinforcers.

Providing Choice

One of the simplest antecedent strategies is to provide choice. This may be as simple as saying "Do you want to do your math problems before snack time or after?" or "Would you prefer to start with independent work or group work?"

Providing choices has been shown to increase on-task behavior in children with autism (Ulke-Kurkcuoglu & Kircaali-Iftar, 2010), reduce aggression in students with severe disabilities (Dyer, Dunlap, & Winterling, 1990), and increase attention to work tasks (Parsons, Reid, Reynolds, & Baumgarner, 1990).

Changing the Demand to Require Less Response Effort

This is another simple antecedent strategy. Perhaps you have a student who begins cursing every time you pass out the graphic organizer for writing a paper. Maybe instead of providing the whole page, you provide the graphic organizer in small parts (such as just the main idea, then just one supporting detail). This indicates that there is a smaller response required before a break is available. Or, you can provide organizers that have starter sentences, so there is not as much for the student to write. Research indicates that decreasing response effort is most effective when combined with other reinforcement strategies (Fischetti, Wilder, Myers, Leon-Enriquez, Sinn, & Rodriguez, 2012).

Visual, Textual, or Vocal/Aural Cues

Visual, textual, or vocal/aural cues are used often in the school setting. These types of cues can come in several forms, including checklists, signs, and visual schedules. For instance, you might put a piece of masking tape on the floor to indicate where the first person in a line should stand, or you might label a basket "homework" so students know where to place their work.

More specifically, textual and audio interventions known as "scripts" have been useful in increasing the social interactions and responses of some learners, serving as prompts to respond to social questions that have been verbally posed by others. Scripts and script fading are described by McClannahan and Krantz (2006) in *Teaching Conversation to Children with Autism: Scripts and Script Fading*. The visual use of texts and auditory use of scripts teach specific conversational skills, initiation skills, and responding skills by systematically presenting short sentences that the learner reads or recites, and then each word is faded systematically until the learner can perform the skill independently (Krantz & McClannahan, 1993; Sarokoff, Taylory, & Poulson, 2001).

Antecedent Strategies: References and Recommended Readings

Cote, C. A., Thompson, R. H., & McKerchar, P. M. (2005). The effects of antecedent interventions and extinction on toddlers' compliance during transitions. *Journal of Applied Behavior Analysis, 38*(2): 235-238.

Dettmer, S., Simpson, R. L., Myles, B. S., & Ganz, J. B. (2000). The use of visual supports to facilitate transitions of students with autism. *Focus on Autism and Other Developmental Disabilities, 15*(3), 163–169.

Dyer, K., Dunlap, G., & Winterling, V. (1990). Effects of choice making on the serious problem behaviors of students with severe handicaps. *Journal of Applied Behavior Analysis, 23*(4), 515-524.

Enloe, K. A., & Rapp, J. T. (2014). Effects of noncontingent social interaction on immediate and subsequent engagement in vocal and motor stereotypy in children with autism. *Behavior Modification, 38*(3),374-391.

Fischetti, A. T., Wilder, D. A., Myers, K., Leon-Enriquez, Y., Sinn, S., & Rodriguez, R. (2012). An evaluation of evidence-based interventions to increase compliance among children with autism. *Journal of Applied Behavior Analysis, 45*(4), 859-863.

Guardino, C. A., & Fullerton, E. (2010). Changing behaviors by changing the classroom environment. *Teaching Exceptional Children, 42*(6), 8-13.

Hanley, G., Piazza, C., & Fisher, W. (1997). Noncontingent presentation of attention and alternative stimuli in the treatment of attention-maintained destructive behavior. *Journal of Applied Behavior Analysis, 30*(2): 229–237.

Krantz, P. J., & McClannahan, L. E. (1993). Teaching children with autism to initiate to peers: Effects of a script-fading procedure. *Journal of Applied Behavior Analysis, 26*(1), 121-132.

McClannahan, L. E., & Krantz, P. J. (2006). *Teaching Conversation to Children with Autism: Scripts and Script Fading.* Bethesda, MD: Woodbine House.

Parsons, M. B., Reid, D. H., Reynolds, J., & Baumgarner, M. (1990). Effects of chosen versus assigned jobs on the work performance of persons with severe handicaps. *Journal of Applied Behavior Analysis, 23*(2), 253-258.

Richling, S. M., Rapp, J. T., Carroll, R. A., Smith, J. N., Nystedt, A., & Siewert, B. (2011). Using noncontingent reinforcement to increase compliance with wearing prescription prostheses. *Journal of Applied Behavior Analysis, 44*(2): 375-379.

Sarokoff, R. A., Taylor, B. A., & Poulson, C. L. (2001). Teaching children with autism to engage in conversational exchanges: Script-fading with embedded textual stimuli. *Journal of Applied Behavior Analysis, 34*(1), 81-84.

Antecedent Strategies: References and Recommended Readings (cont'd)

Twardosz, S., Cataldo, M. F., & Risley, T. R. (1974). Open environment design for infant and toddler day care. *Journal of Applied Behavior Analysis, 7*(4): 529-546.

Ulke-Kurkcuoglu, B., & Kircaali-Iftar, G. (2010). A comparison of the effects of providing activity and material choice to children with autism spectrum disorders. *Journal of Applied Behavior Analysis, 43*(4), 717-721.

Waters, M. B., Lerman, D. C., & Hovanetz, A. N. (2009). Separate and combined effects of visual schedules and extinction plus differential reinforcement on problem behavior occasioned by transitions. *Journal of Applied Behavior Analysis, 42*(2), 309-313.

Wilder, D. A., Chen, L., Atwell, J., Pritchard, J., & Weinstein, P. (2006). Brief functional analysis and treatment of tantrums associated with transitions in preschool children. *Journal of Applied Behavior Analysis, 39*(1), 103-107.

Wilder, D. A., Normand, M., & Attwell, J. (2005). Noncontingent reinforcement as treatment for food refusal and associated self-injury. *Journal of Applied Behavior Analysis, 38*(4), 549-553.

FUNCTIONAL COMMUNICATION TRAINING

Functional communication training (FCT) is perhaps the most powerful antecedent strategy we can use, and probably one of the most researched and effective methods used as an antecedent strategy and behavior reduction procedure (Tiger, Hanley, & Bruzek, 2008). Since its first description by Carr and Durand (1985), FCT has continued to be refined as a function-based treatment in which problem behaviors are addressed. Technically, FCT is a procedure used to reinforce replacement behaviors. In this procedure, one identifies a replacement behavior in advance, then teaches the student to use that replacement behavior to contact the same reinforcement as the original problem behavior. For example, a child that may not have enough language development to communicate effectively may resort to kicking and screaming to obtain a desired edible item from his parents. With FCT, after a thorough functional behavior assessment, a replacement response—such as pointing to a picture card of the item the child wants—is identified to replace the problem behavior. Opportunities to practice this response are set up in analog and natural situations, and the problem behavior does not result in reinforcement. Through intensive training of the new response, problem behaviors decrease and are replaced with functionally equivalent adaptive responses. The table below is reprinted from Tiger, Hanley, and Bruzek's 2008 review of FCT:

Table 1: Best Practice Guidelines for Conducting FCT

When beginning FCT

1. Conduct a functional analysis to identify the reinforcer maintaining problem behavior.
2. Select a communicative response that is recognizable and can be acquired quickly.
3. Identify a trained individual to initiate FCT in a safe, controlled environment.
4. Arrange multiple opportunities to prompt and reinforce the communication response to promote rapid acquisition.
5. Teach the communicative response using most-to-least or least-to-most prompting procedures, and reinforce every instance of the response.
6. Withhold reinforcement for problem behavior and, when necessary, arrange punishers for problem behavior.

Once problem behaviors are reduced in controlled situations

7. Thin the schedule of reinforcement for the communication response by either delaying reinforcer delivery or teaching the client to recognize situations or times when reinforcement is not available for the response.
8. Implement strategies to promote generalization by incorporating multiple trainers or settings into the training, including stimuli from the generalization settings, and conducting training in all relevant contexts.
9. Teach caregivers to respond to communicative and problem behavior.
10. Arrange learning situations in the natural environment.
11. Increase the complexity of the communicative response over time.

Article published in *Behavior Analysis in Practice* in 2008, by Drs. Tiger, Hanley, and Bruzek on FCT. Reprinted/adapted with permission.

Functional Communication Training: References and Recommended Readings

Bird, F., Dores, P. A., Moniz, D., & Robinson, J. (1989). Reducing severe aggressive and self-injurious behaviors with functional communication training. *American Journal of Mental Retardation, 94*(1), 37-48.

Carr E. G., & Durand, V. (1985). Reducing behavior problems through functional communication training. *Journal of Applied Behavior Analysis, 18*(2), 111–126.

Hagopian, L. P., Fisher, W. W., Sullivan, M. T., Acquisto, J., & LeBlanc, L. A. (1998). Effectiveness of functional communication training with and without extinction and punishment: A summary of 21 inpatient cases. *Journal of Applied Behavior Analysis, 31*(2), 211–235.

Tiger, J. H., Hanley, G. P., & Bruzek, J. (2008). Functional communication training: A review and practical guide. *Behavior Analysis in Practice 1*(1), 16-23.

Worsdell, A. S., Iwata, B. A., Hanley, G. P., Thompson, R. H., & Kahng, S. W. (2000). Effects of continuous and intermittent reinforcement for problem behavior during functional communication training. *Journal of Applied Behavior Analysis, 33*(2), 167-79.

ADDRESSING COMMON ISSUES IN DATA COLLECTION

Too Many to Count

Sometimes, teachers or practitioners will decide not to take data on a specific behavior because it occurs at such a high rate they can't accurately count it. There are a few ways to address this:

- Take video of your session so you can count the occurrences of the behavior without also trying to focus on teaching.
- Use whole-interval or partial-interval recording to measure the behavior. (For more on this, see page 13).
- Select a different dimension of the behavior to measure, such as duration or latency.

Targeting Too Many Behaviors

Another common issue is to attempt to measure too many behaviors simultaneously. This increases the likelihood of errors in data collection, and may also increase the frustration or stress of staff attempting to collect so much data. To address this issue:

- Prioritize! Ask yourself: What is the most socially significant behavior I need to address? Start with that first.
- Test your data collection methods and assess for IOA. If you are not achieving high IOA, it's possible there is an issue with your definition of the behavior—but it's also possible that the amount of data you are requiring teachers or practitioners to collect is contributing to errors.

Using the Wrong Tool for Measurement

We've often encountered teachers or practitioners who have only had hands-on training with a few tools for measurement. In such cases, you might see that a tally counter is used to measure every single behavior, or that all teachers are wearing MotivAiders. While we love both of these tools, neither is the right tool in every situation. Refer to page 13 for information on selecting the most appropriate tool for measurement.

Being Responsive to the Data

It's not uncommon to walk into a classroom where a lot of data is being taken, but that data is rarely, if ever, analyzed. The main point of collecting data is to make treatment or teaching decisions based on that data. To address this problem, you might:

- Provide in situ training for collecting then assessing data.
- Set a schedule for daily or weekly assessment of data.
- Provide parameters for how to assess data.

Defining Behavior Accurately

Two common errors with defining behaviors are using vague terms and using terms that are not observable and measureable.

- Identify commonly used vague terms, such as "tantrums" and "noncompliance" and discuss observable and measurable terms that can be used instead.
- Teach about "the dead man's test." If a dead man can do it, then it's not a behavior. For example, you shouldn't target "staying in seat" or "not eating cookies," as a dead man can stay in a seat or not eat cookies.
- Practice the skill of defining behaviors and assess. (Refer to page 28.)

Refining Definitions When Necessary

Part of being responsive to the data is refining the definition when necessary. There are times it may be necessary to refine the definition of a behavior:

- Two or more data collectors are recording very different rates of the behavior.
- The first definition was too broad.

Response Classes By Function:

Behaviors often co-occur, and noticing this is important when developing definitions of behavior. On page 51, we offer an example of Adrian, a preschooler who has tantrums that involve falling to the floor, banging his head, crying, and attempting to bite and aggress toward the teacher? This is an example of a class of behaviors that all serve the same function, which was wanting access to a tangible item (in Adrian's case, trains and cars). Sometimes we might get caught up in wanting to analyze every instance of a response, but that can lead to data collection systems that are cumbersome and susceptible to errors. Question whether several co-occurring responses may be related, in that they all serve the same function. Remember:

- co-occurrence of responses often serve the same function, so
- consider response classes as part of your target behavior definitions, and
- define observable responses as part of the definition.

ACCESSING THE LITERATURE

Throughout the previous chapters, we have tried to embed the utility of accessing the literature. A major tenet of Applied Behavior Analysis is that it is evidence-based. For decades, our field has conducted research about behaviors we can observe in the environment, and has worked to create positive behavior change. But keeping up with research, or determining what is actually evidence-based, can be quite challenging.

One way that some organizations and schools address this issue is by having a "journal club" of sorts. An article is selected each month, the staff read it, and then everyone comes together to discuss it. This is a great way to get people talking about evidence-based procedures, help introduce new concepts, and create an environment that relies on science rather than anecdotal information.

Here are a few tips to get you started:

- **Poll your participants.** What topics might they be interested in? What dates and times work best for them? What is something they want to learn more about? You can use this information to get off on the right foot.
- **Sweeten the meeting.** Make it fun with snacks or themes. It's amazing how free food can draw people in.
- **Create questions for consideration.** When you hand out the article, provide five or six questions for participants to consider as they read. This will help guide their reading and your conversation when you meet.
- **Make it applied.** Think about how the information in the article can be used in your own setting. Have people discuss what it would look like if they tried out the interventions themselves.
- **Ask district to purchase journal.** If none of your staff is affiliated with a university that provides journal subscriptions, you may want to ask your district to purchase a subscription to a journal so you have access to the most up-to-date research.

Finally, take a look at "Reading Groups: A Practical Means of Enhancing Professional Knowledge Among Human Service Practitioners" by Parsons & Reid (2011). This article demonstrates the utility of such groups, as well as important variables for implementing them successfully.

Accessing the Literature: References and Recommended Readings

Parsons, M. B., & Reid, D. H. (2011). Reading groups: A practical means of enhancing professional knowledge among human service practitioners. *Behavior Analysis in Practice, 4*(2), 53-60.

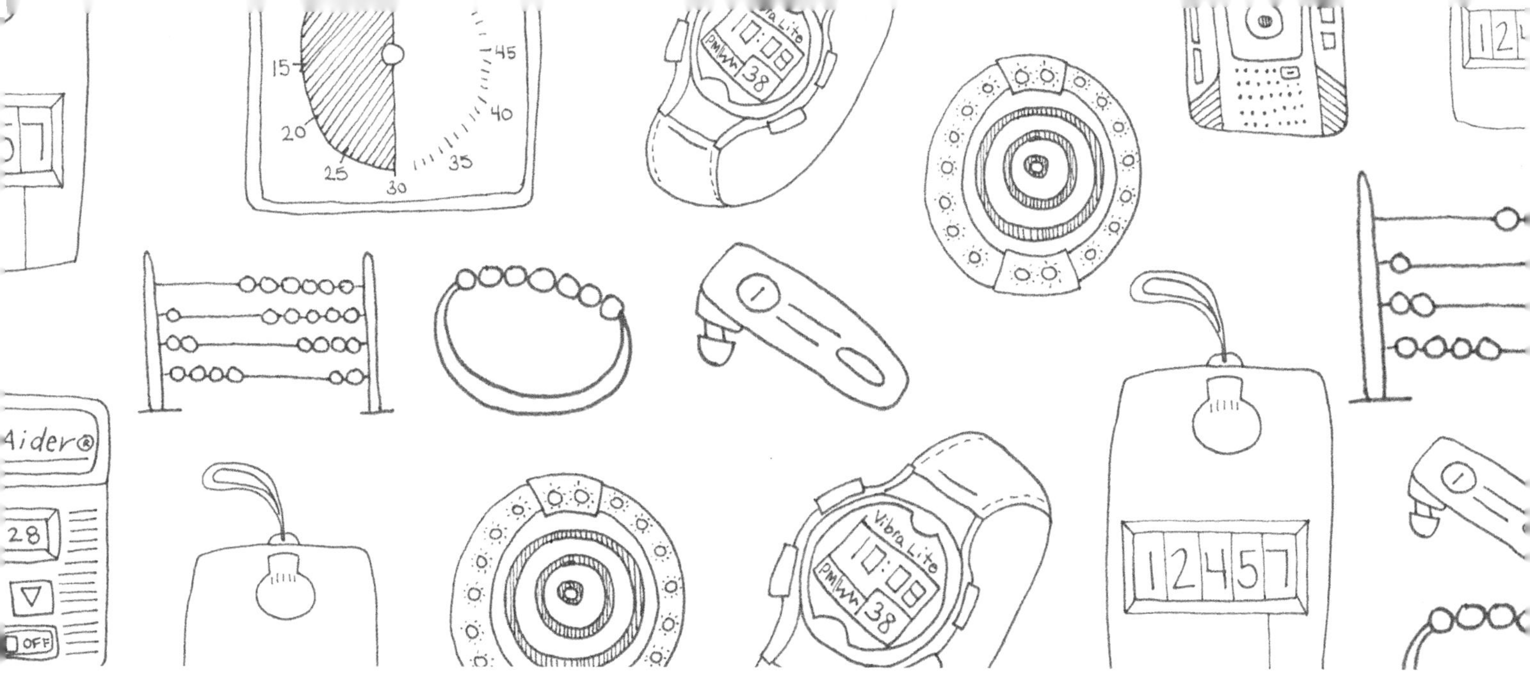

SECTION 4:
Behaviors

How To Use This Section

In this section, you will find behaviors broken down into three main categories:

- Problem Behaviors
- Adaptive Behaviors
- Changing Your Own Behavior

Within each section, we have provided a great deal of content about issues in that category of behavior and evidence-based practice. We have also provided a vignette that highlights one teacher's experience with one of these behaviors. The vignette covers all aspects of identifying and defining the behavior, building an intervention, and using data collection.

When considering how to address a particular behavior, we recommend that you read the appropriate section in its entirety. It will help provide a big-picture view, while also guiding you through the essential steps to creating behavior change. At the end of each section, we have selected related studies that may help you further develop an intervention. We recommend looking at this research, and, if you want more information, looking at the reference sections of these articles for further reading.

Once you have read the content here, go back and think about the phases of data collection. The ultimate goal is to see real progress reflected in the data.

PROBLEM BEHAVIORS

Whether you are a teacher in the classroom, an instructor in the home, or an interventionist working in a day treatment setting, there are several questions you should be asking when the need for intervention arises.

They are:

1. Why do I need to intervene?
2. What is the behavior I am intervening on?
3. How do I go about understanding, tracking, and changing this behavior?

As the word intervention suggests, your goal should be to "interfere" with or disrupt a process. A modification is made to the situation to impact the behavior and hopefully lessen, discontinue, or change it in some way so it is not harmful to the individual or others. "What is harmful?" you may ask. Besides the obvious physical injuries that some problem behaviors may produce, think about the following "harmful" side effects of problem behavior(s), such as self-injury, that may not be as direct (Minshawi, Hurwitz, Fodstad, Biebl, Morris, & McDougle, 2014).

Harmful effects of problem behaviors may:

- evoke negative emotions such as anxiety and fear;
- create environments that do not feel safe (to anyone);
- prevent learning from occurring that is necessary for all students (and all of us);
- contribute to misconceptions of the "intentions" and "motives" of the individual who is struggling with the behaviors; or
- contribute to our own unhelpful biases and beliefs, such as, "some people will never change," or "I can't do anything about it."

With behaviors that are problematic or harmful, we simply want them to stop—and not be repeated for the reasons outlined above. If behaviors are not addressed via evidence-based and empirically proven interventions, several things can happen:

- the problem behavior continues and the person, as well as others around them, continue to get hurt;
- the problem behavior can worsen;
- the individual doesn't learn alterntive or replacement behaviors, and educational opportunities begin to dwindle while problem behaviors become stronger;
- negative emotional reactions (such as anxiety and fear) may continue to occur in individuals expressing the behaviors, as well as those trying to intervene; or
- you feel that you have no control and cannot predict when behaviors will occur again, or believe that you can't do anything about them.

Minshawi, N. F., Hurwitz, S., Fodstad, J. C., Biebl, S., Morriss, D. H., & McDougle, C. J. (2014). The association between self-injurious behaviors and autism spectrum disorders. *Psychology Research and Behavior Management, 7,* 125.

Narrowing it Down

			Problematic Behaviors			
Consider why the behavior is problematic. Typically, it is either a danger to self or others and/or it prevents learning for the individual and/or others.						
Think of the behavior as fitting into one or more of these categories. It will help you fine-tune how you collect data, and conceptualize the behavior in its context. We like to think of these categories.	Disruption	Aggression	Elopement	Pica	Self-injury	Stereotypy
These are some broad definitions to begin with for each category of behavior. Depending on the target behavior, you may need to define specific responses relevant to your learner.	Can be physical or vocal, and disturbs the environment by displacing objects and/or adding noise	Hurts or attempts to hurt others	Leaves a designated area or wanders without permission	Ingests inedible and/or dangerous objects or substances	Hurts or attempts to hurt self	Repetitive and/or non-contextual behavior

COMMON PROBLEM BEHAVIORS

Disruption

Historically, research conducted on disruptive behaviors has included various forms involving motor, vocal, and aggressive behaviors (Thomas, Becker, & Armstrong, 1968). In thinking about the categories of behaviors discussed in this book, we describe disruptive behaviors as instances of behavior in which the environment is qualitatively changed in some way and makes learning for anyone—including the individual whose behavior is being monitored—difficult to accomplish. We have chosen to discuss disruptions in two forms: vocal and physical. Vocal disruptions can range in severity/magnitude, and can come in a variety of forms. A key aspect of vocal disruptions is that the environmental conditions prevent the teacher from teaching and the individual(s) from learning because some vocal noise is produced. Physical disruptions can be any number of responses that affect the physical environment in some way due to another object being displaced in the environment. Physical disruptions also range in severity/magnitude and can come in many forms.

Examples:

- Vocal disruptions include:
  - screaming,
  - swearing/cursing,
  - yelling,
  - incessant noises,
  - talking,
  - crying,
  - laughing,
  - calling out, or
  - coughing.

- Physical disruptions include:
  - swiping materials off one's desk,
  - banging on objects,
  - ripping paper,
  - spilling water,
  - throwing toys,
  - breaking items (e.g., pencils),
  - turning over one's desk,
  - kicking one's chair, or
  - spitting on/at objects (sometimes this can include at others or self).

Vignette: Vocal Disruption

Mrs. Gruebel noticed that Henry was great at raising his hand to answer a question, but if he was not called upon first, he would call out his answer each time. Feedback to not call out didn't seem to work, as it was often given immediately after Henry blurted out an answer. An antecedent intervention of reviewing a social story prior to instruction, one in which raising your hand was required, did not seem to have any effects either. Mrs. Gruebel sought help for this behavior when she noticed other students were missing turns during instruction and Henry had a difficult time waiting to be chosen to respond or not having a turn at all.

Vignette: Physical Disruption

Mrs. Gruebel was often called to respond to Sally, who repeatedly kicked the leg of her chair while sitting at her desk during math instruction. Though Sally did not seem bothered by the kicking, students around her had begun noticing the noise, and voiced that they could not concentrate on their reading. Despite asking Sally repeatedly to stop banging her leg, after a short cessation of the behavior, she would reliably resume once the teacher walked away to help other students.

Special Considerations

It is possible that physical disruptions can also result in inadvertent injury or harm to someone. However, if that is a typical response that is observed, our preference would be to include it under aggression (in which harm is toward someone else) or self-injury (in which harm is toward the self). The key definitional distinction is that physical disruptions do not include aggression and self-injury, but prevent learning in some way; the behavior interrupts learning or does not allow it to continue.

Know your class environment: perhaps all your students call out constantly, and it is something you would like to see decrease as a whole in the class. If this is the case, you may want a classroom-wide management system. Or, you may be in a situation where one or two students seem to affect one or two other students, creating a smaller group that needs an intervention.

I want this behavior to decrease because it interferes with learning.	Disruptions (vocal or physical responses that interfere with learning)			
Step 1: What dimension of the behavior can you measure?	Can you count it as an instance of a response?	Can you measure the duration of the behavior? Is the duration important?	Can you measure when the behavior occurs in relation to other events?	Are there any other dimensions you need to consider?
Step 2: Write your definition, including all relevant dimensions	Example 1: Vocal disruption is defined as any vocalization above speaking volume, using swear words and/or words that are belittling to others, and occuring during academic tasks such as math and reading. This does not include the individual's reading belittling words in books aloud. Belittling examples include "You're so stupid, you're nothing," and so on.			
	Example 2: Physical disruption is defined as any instance in which the individual throws, shoves, grabs, or pushes his work materials off the desk or out of his teacher's hands during instruction.			

Potential Tools

Measuring noises, profanity, stomping of the feet, or other types of disruptions we have discussed often involves using a data sheet uniquely created for these behaviors, a MotivAider to prompt you to measure time samples of the behaviors (especially if the behavior is of a high-frequency nature), and a pencil. If the behavior is low frequency, a simple counter or a piece of masking tape to tally it will suffice. Afterward, you can transfer information you counted to the data sheet. If dimensions of the behavior indicate high rates, you may resort to time-sampling procedures with specified times of the day and durations in which you collect data. You would need a timer, data sheet, pencil, and possibly a counter and MotivAider.

Disruptions: References and Recommended Readings

Donaldson, J. M., & Vollmer, T. R. (2011). An evaluation and comparison of time-out procedures with and without release contingencies. *Journal of Applied Behavior Analysis, 44*(4), 693-705.

Kennedy, C. H., & Itkonen, T. (1993). Effects of setting events on the problem behavior of students with severe disabilities. *Journal of Applied Behavior Analysis, 26*(3), 321-327.

Piazza, C. C., Moes, D. R., & Fisher, W. W. (1996). Differential reinforcement of alternative behavior and demand fading in the treatment of escape-maintained destructive behavior. *Journal of Applied Behavior Analysis, 29*(4), 569-572.

Thomas, D. R., Becker, W. C., & Armstrong, M. (1968). Production and elimination of disruptive classroom behavior by systematically varying teacher's behavior. *Journal of Applied Behavior Analysis, 1*(1), 35-45.

AGGRESSION

Aggressions as problem behavior are abundantly referred to in the research literature, and are primarily thought of as learned behavior (Marcus, Vollmer, Swanson, Roane, & Ringdahl, 2001). Aggression can vary in form and range in severity, and is often a high priority for intervention no matter the severity. We define aggression generally as any instance or attempt at physically engaging in a harmful or potentially harmful action toward someone, and/or using any object to do the same toward another person in which physical contact occurs. For each form of aggression, it is highly recommended that the responses are defined, based on your learner(s).

Examples:

- hitting,
- biting,
- scratching,
- striking,
- kicking,
- pushing,
- shoving,
- slapping, or
- punching.

Vignette: A Preschooler Having a Tantrum

Adrian recently began attending a preschool disabilities class for children on the spectrum. Within the first day, the teacher noticed that any time Adrian had to put car toys and trains away, he would fall to the floor, bang his head, and cry uncontrollably for several minutes. When the teacher went over to pick up Adrian and prevent him from banging his head, he would aggress toward her, try to bite, and continue to cry. Adrian was unable to join his peers to sit at a center for pre-writing skills. Although Adrian could make basic needs known—such as asking for preferred items and things to eat—he was unable to make his needs known under conditions in which he had to relinquish highly preferred toys and transition to non-preferred tasks such as writing and coloring.

Mrs. Stone, Adrian's teacher, quickly understood that she needed to address the behaviors before they worsened. She was most concerned about the head-banging and biting. With the help of the behavior analyst, she quickly defined Adrian's behavior as a tantrum, making sure to incorporate the responses of head bangs and bites into her operational definition. For tools, they used a timer, counter, ABC data sheet, and a frequency and duration data sheet to measure both the number of head bangs and bites as well as the duration of the tantrum episodes. This was hard because Mrs. Stone had several other students to attend to, and when tantrums started, she wasn't always able to grab a timer and begin measuring duration. Often she would look at the clock above her door while trying to block any head bangs or bites, and wait for Adrian's tantrum to de-escalate. Duration data was recorded on the data sheet immediately after the tantrum behavior was over for at least one minute. Bites and head bangs were tallied on two different color counters (red for bites, and silver for head bangs) attached to Mrs. Stone's belt loop, and then transferred to the data sheet once the tantrum was over.

After the behavior analyst and Mrs. Stone completed the FBA and determined that the behavior was driven by access to tangibles (denied access function) and compounded by difficult work that followed periods in which preferred items had to be relinquished, a behavior intervention plan was set up to address skill deficits, transitions, and functional communication use.

Special Considerations

When aggressions is concern, the things we always want to do first are interrupt it, block it, and discontinue it immediately if it is ongoing in the moment. Interrupting aggression is often difficult in public school settings, because it may occur and the person aggressing may stop on his/her own before you get to him or her. Blocking, though often recommended, is difficult to do when the behavior is not ongoing. We may not be able to respond in time to prevent an aggression from occurring, depending on where we are physically in the room. It is often necessary to find ways to change environmental conditions under which aggression may occur, as well as assessing and reinforcing precursor behaviors that may lead to the aggression. For example, if you determine that yelling is a precursor to aggression, reinforce the yelling initially before it escalates to aggression. Once you determine what the precursors are, you will be in a better position to identify alternative behaviors to teach using functional communication training and differential reinforcement procedures.

Some basic strategies to think about for less severe aggressive behavior involve engineering the environment so that it is harder for aggression to be efficient and also prevents others from getting hurt. For example, put barriers between the child that aggresses and others—such as a desk, distance between two people, a teacher between two students, or seating that is not within reach of others.

With severe forms of aggression, training in crisis prevention and response is critical. Organizations such as Safety-Care™ by QBS, Inc. provide excellent behaviorally-based training to deal with addressing a behavioral crisis.

I want this behavior to decrease because it is harmful.	## Aggression (hurting or attempting to hurt others)			
Step 1: What dimension of the behavior can you measure?	Can you count the behavior as an instance of a response?	Is the magnitude (force or intensity) of this behavior important to measure?	Can you measure the duration of the behavior? Is it important to measure?	Can you measure *when* the behavior occurs in relation to other events? For example, what is the response latency or inter-response time of the behavior?
Step 2: Write your definition. What does the behavior look like (form)?	Aggression is defined as any instance in which John Doe attempts to, or succeeds in, biting another person. Biting is defined as any instance in which John Doe's teeth make contact with the skin or clothing of another person.			

Potential Tools

- Data Sheets that are carefully constructed and cue the observer to record information accurately based on dimensions of behavior and definition that has been developed
- Timers
- Counters
- MotivAider
- Visual Time Timer

Aggression: References and Recommended Readings

Carr, E. G., Newsom, C. D., & Binkoff, J. A. (1980). Escape as a factor in the aggressive behavior of two retarded children. *Journal of Applied Behavior Analysis, 13*(1), 101-117.

Marcus, B. A., Vollmer, T. R., Swanson, V., Roane, H. R., & Ringdahl, J. E. (2001). An experimental analysis of aggression. *Behavior Modification 25*(2), 189-213.

Murphy, H. A., Hutchison, J. M., & Bailey, J. S. (1983). Behavioral school psychology goes outdoors: The effect of organized games on playground aggression. *Journal of Applied Behavior Analysis, 16*(1), 29-35.

Thompson, R. H., Fisher, W. W., Piazza, C. C., & Kuhn, D. E. (1998). The evaluation and treatment of aggression maintained by attention and automatic reinforcement. *Journal of Applied Behavior Analysis, 31*(1), 103-116.

ELOPEMENT

Elopement is running away, wandering, bolting, or leaving a designated area under supervision without consent. Elopement can occur in school settings, in the home, or in public settings, and is considered one of the most concerning behaviors in individuals with autism (Autism New Jersey, 2014). While it can also be seen as a disruptive behavior (such as when a student runs out of a classroom), elopement is also an incredibly dangerous behavior that presents enormous safety risks to the individual, such as drowning or vehicle accidents. It is a significant source of stress many families face, contributing to a lowered quality of life, living under constant stress (Autism New Jersey, 2014). Some researchers have identified two specific forms of elopement, describing them as: goal-directed bolting and wandering (Fisher & Bowen, 2014). Goal-directed bolting typically involves leaving a supervised area to pursue something attractive or obtain a desired item, whereas wandering involves moving about aimlessly, without a clear goal or destination (Fisher & Bowen, 2014). Though more research on elopement is critically needed, the research that does exist has shown that the function of elopement varies from individual to individual (Lang, R., Rispoli, M., Machalicek, W., White, P. J., Kang, S., Pierce, N., Mulloy, A., Fragale, T., O'Reilly, M., Sigafoos, J., & Lancioni, G., 2009), and it is therefore imperative to do a functional analysis of elopement prior to implementing an intervention (Piazza, Hanley, Bowman, Ruyter, Lindauer, & Saiontz, 1997; Lang, R., Davis, T., O'Reilly, M., Machalicek, W., Rispoli, M., Sigafoos, J., Lancioni, G., & Regester, A., 2010).

Examples:
- Running out of the classroom (or any setting where person is under supervision).
- Leaving the house without permission.
- Bolting/running toward a desired item/activity (food, toys, pool, sprinklers, playground) without permission.
- Wandering from a crowded/busy area (e.g., gym, class activity, supermarket, fair).

Vignette: Elopement

Flora, a 5th grade student with autism and intellectual disability was always fascinated by watches that others wore on their wrist. She would often dart to a complete stranger and grab their wrist to look at the watch. One of her favorite things to do was to say how pretty the watch was and then feel the strap for texture. Not surprisingly, this was a behavior that teachers and parents equally were concerned about since Flora has startled many an innocent bystander who was grabbed at the wrist when entering a restaurant or walking in the community. Flora's behavior can be considered goal-directed bolting because she would "run off" only when she saw the attractive objects she liked.

To address the goal directed bolting, Flora's intervention team worked on decreasing Flora's motivation to engage in the behavior as well as training functional communication skills such as initiating with a caregiver if she could go approach a known individual who was wearing a watch. Flora was reinforced by being allowed to approach the person and then was required to comment to the person that she liked their watch, before touching it. After that, she was required to ask if she could touch the watch (similar how you might teach a young child if they can pet someone's dog). Once the functional requests were established, Flora was then taught to accept "no" when she requested to touch the watch, or approach someone with a watch or comment about it. A systematic chain of behaviors to address each step in the goal-directed bolting was critical in first establishing appropriate forms of communication but also working with Flora's strong interest and motivation regarding watches. The final step included teaching Flora to discriminate between known people and strangers and to accept "no" when wanting to go touch watches of strangers.

Special Consideration

- Have a safety plan if your student engages in elopement and share it with law enforcement and/or other community members.
- Make sure an FBA on elopement has been conducted, and a thorough behavior intervention plan is included in the Individualized Education Plan for your child.
- Encourage training of local firefighters and police about children with autism.
- Intervening early: If you have a student who runs to the door but never runs out, intervene then. You don't want the behavior to be inadvertently shaped to a more dangerous behavior, such as actually running out of the classroom or the building.

I want to decrease this behavior because it is dangerous and puts the individual at risk for harm.		Elopement (running away, wandering, bolting, or leaving a designated area under supervision without consent)		
Step 1: What dimension of the behavior can you measure?	Can you count it as an instance of a response?	Is the magnitude (force or intensity) of this behavior important to measure?	Can you measure the duration of the behavior? Is it important to measure?	Can you measure *when* the behavior occurs in relation to other events? For example, what is the response latency or inter-response time of the behavior?
Step 2: Write your definition. What does the behavior look like (form)?		Example 1: Elopement is defined as Flora bolting from a designated location to a person (known or unknown) who may be wearing a watch or similar object on their wrist. Bolting distance is at least ten feet.		
		Example 2: Elopement is defined as Johnny leaving the designated area through a door (i.e. front door, classroom door) and wandering without supervision.		

Potential Tools

- Tracking apps on phones, such as FindFriends on the iPhone or GPS Phone Tracker Pro for Android
- Tracking devices (bracelets, tags in clothes), such as those provided through Project Lifesaver
- Identification with contact information (temporary tattoos, ID cards, labeled clothing with identifying information)

Elopement: References and Recommended Readings

Autism New Jersey, (2014). Elopement and Wandering: Your guide to safety resources. [Pamphlet]. Robbinsville, NJ: Autism New Jersey.

Call, N. A., Pabico, R. S., Findley, A. J., & Valentino, A. L. (2011). Differential reinforcement with and without blocking as treatment for elopement. *Journal of Applied Behavior Analysis, 44*(4), 903-907.

Falcomata, T. S., Roane, H. S., Feeney, B. J., & Stephenson, K. M. (2010). Assessment and treatment of elopement maintained by access to stereotypy. *Journal of Applied Behavior Analysis, 43*(3), 513-517.

Fisher. W., & Bowen, M. (2014, July). An Empirical Model for Individualized Assessment and Treatment of Two Types of Elopement: Goal-Directed Bolting and Aimless Wandering. Paper presented at the meeting of National Autism Conference, State College/University Park, PA.

Lang, R., Rispoli, M., Machalicek, W., White, P. J., Kang, S., Pierce, N., Mulloy, A., Fragale, T., O'Reilly, M., Sigafoos, J., & Lancioni, G. (2009). Treatment of elopement in individuals with developmental disabilities: A systematic review. *Research in Developmental Disabilities, 30*(4), 670-681.

Lang, R., Davis, T., O'Reilly, M., Machalicek, W., Rispoli, M., Sigafoos, J., Lancioni, G., & Regester, A. (2010). Functional analysis and treatment of elopement across two school settings. *Journal of Applied Behavior Analysis, 43*(1), 113-118.

Piazza, C. C., Hanley, G. P., Bowman, L. G., Ruyter, J. M., Lindauer, S. E., & Saiontz, D. M. (1997). Functional analysis and treatment of elopement. *Journal of Applied Behavior Analysis, 30*(4), 653-672.

Tarbox, R. S .F., Wallace, M., & Williams, L. (2003). Assessment and Treatment of Elopement: A replication and extension. *Journal of Applied Behavior Analysis 36*(2), 239-244.

SELF-INJURY

Self-injurious behavior can range from mild to very intense injury causing permanent physical harm and, in rare cases, death. When intense, it can be disturbing to observe, especially if it is your first time witnessing self-injury. It is not uncommon to feel scared, anxious, and sometimes unsure of what to do, even if you have dealt with the behavior before. As with other behaviors that can harm the self, you will always want to try to prevent it, stop it, or interrupt it as immediately as possible. Self-injury is defined as any behavior that physically harms or has the potential of harming one's self both immediately and long-term.

Examples:
- head banging,
- head hitting,
- biting self,
- scratching self,
- hitting self with fist,
- hitting self with an object,
- dangerous climbing, or
- ingesting non-edible substances or dangerous substances (pills, toxic levels of medication).

Vignette: Self-Injury

Ms. Sue has noticed that when Sarah does not get what she wants, she will hit herself on the head with her hand, and then fall to the floor continuing to bang her legs and feet. One day she reportedly fell to the floor and picked up her head and slammed it on the carpeted floor. She was about to do it again when the para-educator interrupted her by instinctively placing her hand under her head and then pulling the child up to a seated position.

Special Considerations

In a self-contained classroom, it is not unusual to see mild to moderate forms of self-injurious behavior. It is critical that such behavior is analyzed using functional behavior assessment procedures. Too often, behavior that is mild develops into stronger behavior because it was not intervened on early and consistently. This may happen because of the "mild nature" of the behavior; a teacher or professional may not be aware of the potential of the behavior strengthening over time, possibly growing worse without formal intervention. Behavior intervention plans that are function-based are necessary to address self-injury, particularly if you are not sure why the behavior is happening. A consultation by an experienced BCBA who can conduct an FBA and create a behavior intervention plan (BIP) based on function will be very important.

With self-injurious behavior, you may also be able to identify precursor behaviors. For instance, perhaps before attempting to bite his own hand, John often begins tapping his hand rapidly on his knee. It may be possible to do a functional analysis of this hand-tapping behavior and intervene *before* SIB occurs.

I want this behavior to decrease because it is physically damaging and hurts my student.	# Self-Injury (any response that is physically harmful to oneself)			
Step 1: What dimension of the behavior can you measure?	Can you count it as an instance of a response?	Can you measure the duration of the behavior? Is it important?	Can you measure when the behavior occurs in relation to other events?	Is the magnitude (force or intensity of the behavior) important for data collection?
Step 2: What does your behavior look like? Write a measurable definition.	Example 1: Head banging: Any instance in which Sara's head makes contact with a hard surface such as the wall or desk from a distance of six inches or more. Head banging does not include instances in which Sarah is resting her head on the table surface.			
	Example 2: Leveled definition to include intensity/magnitude. Level 1: Above definition; Level 2: More than two repetitive head hits in a row; Level 3: Head banging resulting in redness, swelling, bruising, or bleeding anywhere on the head.			

Potential Tools

- Data Sheet specifically tailored to definition (cue the data collector to take accurate data)
- Timer
- Counter
- MotivAider
- ImageJ software for measuring wound size area

Self-Injury: References and Recommended Readings

Dracobly, J. D., & Smith, R. G. (2012). Progressing from identification and functional analysis of precursor behavior to treatment of self-injurious behavior. *Journal of Applied Behavior Analysis, 45*(2), 361-374.

Kurtz, P. F., Chin, M. D., Huete, J. M., Tarbox, R. S., O'Connor, J. T., Paclawskyj, T. R., & Rush, K. S. (2003). Functional analysis and treatment of self-injurious behavior in young children: A summary of 30 cases. *Journal of Applied Behavior Analysis, 36*(2), 205-219.

McCord, B. E., Thomson, R. J., & Iwata, B. A. (2001). Functional analysis and treatment of self-injury associated with transitions. *Journal of Applied Behavior Analysis, 34*(2), 195-210.

Minshawi, N. R., Hurwitz, S., Fodstad, J. C., Beibl, S., Morriss, D. H., & McDougle, C. J. (2014). The association between self-injurious behaviors and autism spectrum disorders. *Psychology Research and Behavior Management, 7*, 125-136.

Zarcone, J. R., Iwata, B. A., Vollmer, T. R., Jagtiani, S., Smith, R. G., & Mazaleski, J. L. (1993). Extinction of self-injurious escape behavior with and without instructional fading. *Journal of Applied Behavior Analysis, 26*(3), 353-360.

Pica (A form of Self-Injurious Behavior)

Pica is simply defined as eating or mouthing non-nutritive substances. Substances can be dangerous and/or lead to various medical issues and even death (depending on the substance). Examples of pica in individuals with developmental disabilities have included: paper clips, cigarette butts, paper, rocks, string, paint chips, Play-Doh, antibacterial sanitizer and liquid soaps, toothpaste, and other substances.

Examples:
- actively searching for non-nutritive substances,
- mouthing toys and/or non-food items, or
- swallowing non-food items.

Vignette: Pica

Natalie attended a highly specialized ABA program. A significant problem behavior in her repertoire consisted of mouthing toys and licking/drinking antibacterial sanitizer and soaps. Natalie was very quick. When washing her hands, her teacher would have to stay right by her side to prevent and/or interrupt Natalie from dispensing the soap and then licking it immediately before rubbing her hands together for washing. While walking in the hallways, Natalie needed to be monitored closely because she would quickly run to the area where sanitizer was kept, dispense it, and lick it. One time she was caught opening a sanitizer pump and putting her mouth to the bottle ready to drink it.

Natalie also loved the taste of various sodas, like Coke or Pepsi. After a thorough assessment involving a functional analysis, it was determined that Natalie's pica functioned to obtain highly preferred flavors in liquid form. An intervention was set up in which Natalie had access to various soda flavors, Jell-O, and flavored waters contingent on functional communication for those items while she worked. Interventions also included blocking and systematic exposure to the pica items in the environment. For example, every time Natalie had to walk down the hallway where the sanitizer dispenser was mounted, staff ensured that any attempts to access the sanitizer were initially blocked. Then slowly, she was allowed to pump a very small amount and immediately prompted to rub the sanitizer in her hands, while her hands were blocked from entering her mouth, and competing reinforcement was provided in the form of a soda drink. The same procedures were followed when Natalie went to the bathroom and had access to liquid soap. Staff also ensured that that non-scented soaps and sanitizers were used around the facility to lessen the motivation for Natalie to engage in the behavior.

As you can imagine, the intervention is intense and requires a lot of vigilance. Data collection included measuring the frequency of Natalie's behavior, which included any mouthing, licking, and/or ingestion of non-edible substances throughout the school day, as well as any attempts of the behaviors.

Special Considerations

For individuals engaging in pica-related behaviors, we suggest:
- blocking all attempts of the individual to put items in mouth,
- distracting individual away from potential substance to be mouthed or ingested,
- ensuring that environment is free from known dangerous substances, and
- monitoring and observing the individual at all times.

I want to stop this behavior because it is harmful to my student.	## Pica 			
	(eating or mouthing non-nutritive substances) 			
Step 1: What dimension of the behavior can you measure?	Can you count it as an instance of a response?	Can you measure the duration of the behavior? Is it important?	Can you measure when the behavior occurs in relation to other events?	Is the magnitude (force or intensity of the behavior) important for data collection?
Step 2: What does your behavior look like? Write a measurable definition.	Example 1: Any instance in which Natalie licks and/or ingests hand sanitizer. 			
	Example 2: Any instance in which Zak attempts to or succeeds in mouthing, licking, or ingesting paper clips or any other form of metal. 			

Potential Tools

- Paper and pencil for tallying
- Counter
- Masking tape
- MotivAider

Pica: References and Recommended Readings

Anna, D., Roane, H. S., & Veenstra, R. A. (2011). Functional analysis and treatment of coprophagia. *Journal of Applied Behavior Analysis, 44*(1), 151-155.

Call, N. A., Simmons, C.A., Lomas Mevers, J. E., & Alvarez, J. P. (2015). Clinical outcomes of behavioral treatments for pica in children with developmental disabilities. *Journal of Autism and Developmental Disorders, 45*(7), 2105-2114.

McCord, B. E., Grosser, J. W., Iwata, B. A., & Powers, L. A. (2005). An analysis of response blocking parameters in the prevention of pica. *Journal of Applied Behavior Analysis, 38*(3), 391-394.

STEREOTYPY

The science literature defines stereotypy as behavior that occurs repetitively, rigidly, is invariant, and is often inappropriate in nature, due to developmental and social inappropriateness when compared to age (Cunningham & Schreibman, 2008). It can involve many forms of responses including vocal and motor behavior, with or without objects. When vocal forms of stereotypy occur, it can involve language that is repetitive and/or restrictive, there may be an insistence on sameness or inflexibility with routine, and others. Stereotypy can be simple or complex, and is often quite heterogeneous in form (how it looks). More importantly, function may play a critical role when intervening on stereotypy in that social contingencies, as well as automatically maintaining contingencies, may reinforce the behaviors. The literature on stereotypy has distinguished a subcategory of stereotypy known as self-stimulatory behavior (SSB) (Cunningham & Schreibman, 2008). Unlike stereotypy, which may have various functions, self-stimulatory behavior often carries the implication of an automatic function, which means that the behavior response is the same as the reinforcer.

Examples:

- motor movements with foot/hand/body (e.g., flapping, flicking fingers, rocking);
- scripting;
- blinking/squinting;
- carrying items around;
- lining things up; or
- visual examination of objects, such as using peripheral vision.

Vignette: Stereotypy

Ms. Viscotti had developed a behavioral system to help Sandy deal with her rocking behavior during circle time in which greetings, calendar review, and ABCs were the goals for all preschoolers. Sandy regularly sat at circle and within seconds would engage in vigorous rocking of her body back and forth while her arms flared to the sides. This was quite noticeable to peers, which made Sandy stand out, and often interfered with discussions in the class. To intervene, Ms. Viscotti offered a rocking chair that Sandy could sit in during circle time. This way, she had the opportunity to rock back and forth while the discussions continued. An immediate effect was that Sandy did not stand out from her peers and she was able to immediately stop and answer questions when necessary. Other students were impacted positively as distractions of rocking decreased.

Special Considerations

- You need to ask yourself about the social validity of addressing stereotypy. Sometimes stereotypy interferes with an individual's ability to learn, and therefore it should be addressed. However, there are times when stereotypy is intervened upon to meet another person's needs, such as when a teacher finds it annoying or bothersome. In those cases, you need to be sure that addressing stereotypy is actually a valid intervention.

- Stereotypy should be thought of as occurring to some degree in all people. Having the mindset that we should not aim to completely extinguish stereotypy allows us to understand and accept that minimizing its occurrence during times when it is most disruptive, harmful, or inappropriate is the goal we ought to have and is acceptable.

- Understanding that stereotypy is perhaps one of the most difficult behaviors to address when it occurs as a self-stimulatory behavior (SSB) is very important, because it is the actual behavior (e.g., hand flapping) that also serves as the reinforcer for the behavior, and often it is a behavior that is highly expert in the individual. That is, they are really good at engaging in the behavior, and it has been reinforced every single time.

- The intervention must be based on the function of the behavior. Often people assume that stereotypy occurs as a symptom of autism and therefore is controlled by some internal, unviewable source. However, there are instances of stereotypy that function for attention or escape. Stereotypy should be assessed just as any other behavior would be assessed prior to intervention.

- Once you have assessed, consider functionally-equivalent replacement behaviors that can be taught, as well as possibilities for differential reinforcement of alternative or incompatible behaviors.
- Stereotypy as a response is not specific to autism; it occurs in many young children and across various developmental disabilities. Stereotypy is also often correlated to environments that are absent of stimulation and sensory enrichment. For example, many case studies have examined orphanages in Romania, in which children were deprived of any type of stimulation (toys, games, social interactions) and, as a result, engaged in high rates of stereotypic behaviors (Bos, Zeanah, Smyke, Fox, & Nelson, 2010; Fisher, Ames, Chisholm, & Savoie, 1997; Mason, 2006).

I want this behavior to decrease because it interferes with learning.	**Stereotypy** (a repetitive, nonfunctional behavior)			
Step 1: What dimension of the behavior can you measure?	Can you count it as an instance of a response?	Can you measure the duration of the behavior? Is it important?	Can you measure when the behavior occurs in relation to other events?	Is the magnitude (force or intensity of the behavior) important for data collection?
Step 2: What does your behavior look like? Write a measurable definition.	Stereotypy is defined as a repetitive, nonfunctional behavior and can take various forms: Example 1: Visual Stereotypy: Any instance in which Adrian directs his peripheral gaze toward the corner of his eyes, blinks for three or more seconds, and/or examines objects or hands very closely (two inches from object). Example 2: Motor/Tactile Stereotypy: Any instance in which Adrian repeatedly, more than two times, moves his torso in a back and forth manner while standing with legs apart or sitting on a chair. Example 3: Vocal Stereotypy: Any instance in which Adrian repeats the same word, phrase, or sound more than two times.			

Potential Tools

- Data Sheet
- Timer
- MotivAider

Stereotypy References and Recommended Readings

Ahearn, W. H., Clark, K. M., MacDonald, R. P., & Chung, B. I. (2007). Assessing and treating vocal stereotypy in children with autism. *Journal of Applied Behavior Analysis, 40*(2), 263-275.

Ahrens, E. N., Lerman, D. C., Kodak, T., Worsdell, A. S., & Keegan, C. (2011). Further evaluation of response interruption and redirection as treatment for stereotypy. *Journal of Applied Behavior Analysis, 44*(1), 95-108.

Bos, K. J., Zeanah, C. H., Smyke, A. T., Fox, N. A., & Nelson, C. A. (2010). Stereotypies in children with a history of early institutional care. *Archives of Pediatrics & Adolescent Medicine, 164*(5), 406-411.

Cunningham, A. B., & Schreibman, L. (2008). Stereotypy and Autism: The importance of function. *Research in Autism Spectrum Disorders, 2*(3): 469-479.

Dib, N., & Sturmey, P. (2007). Reducing student stereotypy by improving teachers' implementation of discrete-trial teaching. *Journal of Applied Behavior Analysis, 40*(2), 339-343.

Fisher, L., Ames, E. W., Chisholm, K., & Savoie, L. (1997). Problems reported by parents of Romanian orphans adopted to British Columbia. *International Journal of Behavioral Development, 20*(1), 67-82

Kennedy, C. H., Meyer, K. A., Knowles, T., & Shukla, S. (2000). Analyzing the multiple functions of stereotypical behavior for students with autism: Implications for assessment and treatment. *Journal of Applied Behavior Analysis, 33*(4), 559-571.

Lang, R., O'Reilly, M., Sigafoos, J., Machalicek, W., Rispoli, M., Lancioni, G. E., & Fragale, C. (2010). The effects of an abolishing operation intervention component on play skills, challenging behavior, and stereotypy. *Behavior Modification, 34*(4), 267-289.

Mason, G. J. (2006). Deprivation stereotypies in human children: The case of the Romanian orphans. Stereotypic Behaviour in Captive Animals: Fundamentals and Applications to Welfare.

Woo, C. C., & Leon, M. (2013). Environmental enrichment as an effective treatment for autism: A randomized controlled trial. *Behavioral Neuroscience, 127*(4), 487-497.

Woo, C. C., Donnelly, J. H., Steinberg-Epstein, R., & Leon, M. (2015). Environmental enrichment as a therapy for autism: A clinical trial replication and extension. *Behavioral Neuroscience, 129*(4), 412.

ADAPTIVE BEHAVIORS

Often in the course of addressing deficits, we may forget to build on strengths or focus on adaptive skills. It's important to ask ourselves what our students *can* do, so that we build into programming and curriculum opportunities to develop skills and adaptive behaviors.

Adaptive skills not only help students become more independent, but have the potential to improve our students' quality of life. But in an era in which the focus of education is on testing and academic outcomes, these essential skills often fall by the wayside. Math, reading, and other core subjects are still very important, but our students need additional work in pivotal skills, self-help skills, and leisure skills. The question then becomes "How do you build lessons in these key skill areas into an already packed daily schedule?"

One of the simplest ways is to incorporate these skills into your behavior intervention plans. An essential component of any strong intervention is a replacement behavior for the undesirable behavior. The skills listed in this section provide a starting point for identifying replacement behaviors that are effective in reducing other problem behaviors and lead to further skill development. In addition, creating clearly defined replacement behaviors provides more opportunities for your student to contact reinforcement for desirable behaviors. It can change the focus of your classroom from one that focuses on decreasing inappropriate behaviors to one that focuses on increasing appropriate behaviors. While this may seem like subtle wordplay, it can make a huge difference in the classroom environment.

Another way to increase the time you spend addressing adaptive behaviors is to change some of your own behaviors as a teacher. We'll discuss this in further detail in the next chapter.

AIMING FOR INDEPENDENCE

Adaptive Behaviors

Adaptive behavior is essential for survival and independence, and will increase the quality of life for the individual. After a thorough assessment, consider the adaptive skills that need to be taught to each individual.

We love these categories because they highlight some core areas of skills needed for independence and quality of life. Often, they can be selected as replacement behavior for the problematic behavior you are trying to decrease.	Pivotal	Self-help	Leisure
These are some broad behaviors to think about when honing in on replacement behaviors, as well as skill deficits. Defining and knowing how to measure these behaviors are critical to developing these skills.	Communication	Self-care	Self-management/ self-monitoring
	Flexibility	Choice-making	
	Responsiveness	Schedule-following	

PIVOTAL SKILLS

Pivotal behaviors are those that, when targeted, will affect other behaviors in a broader and collateral way. Pivotal behaviors allow the learner to acquire new skills without directly targeting them (Koegel & Koegel, 2006). For example, targeting the ability to scan items can be considered a pivotal behavior because scanning is used in several other skills such as reading, discrimination, or searching for an item. Another example is learning to initiate and mand for desired items by targeting motivation as a pivotal skill. Motivation is required for any type of mand, and would be considered a pivotal skill because other types of requests can be taught when motivation is assessed and used (e.g. mand for desired items, for missing items, or for information). Finally, responding to multiple cues in the environment is beneficial for all learners as it sets the stage for attending to various stimuli including words.

Motivation

No discussion of pivotal behaviors is complete without an analysis of motivation. Motivation in behavior analysis is a concept integral to every assessment of behavior and intervention that one might conduct. This includes physical observable behaviors as well as language or "Verbal Behavior" (Skinner, 1953; 1957). Skinner (1953) described the variables of satiation and deprivation when discussing motivation, stating that these variables increase or decrease the likelihood of responses related to the primary reinforcers associated with those responses. The term *motivation* is now used to describe the idea that consequences of behavior are influenced based on the deprivation or satiation state of the individual and/or organism.

A very important point that Skinner made was that satiation and deprivation were more than just the physical or physiological events that can be affected, such as thirst or hunger. An example of a nontangible motivational variable might be social attention. If you increase the deprivation of social attention, responses that obtain social attention are more likely to occur. Skinner also discussed motivation in terms of language and how we learn to request (1957). Not only did Skinner acknowledge that motivation is important in learning various behaviors, but also stated that the learning of language is no different in terms of the principles of behavior, such as antecedents and consequences that affect behavior.

Language, according to Skinner had one special property: it involves the social interaction between speakers and listeners (Sundberg & Michael, 2001; Sundberg, 2008), and both "speaker" behaviors and "listener" behaviors are discrete and learned. With language, Skinner (1957) stressed that both form (how we communicate, such as speaking, writing, using various parts of speech like nouns, verbs, or prepositions) and function (why we communicate or use those specific words, signs, or gestures) are equally important in the study of language. That is, the requests or mands we make are directly influenced by motivation for the requested tangible item or information (Skinner, 1957). For example, If I'm lost on a New York City street (motivation is high for getting help on how to get to my destination), I can ask a passerby how to get to Penn Station using the subway (my response, asking for information) and the passerby tells me to take the 2 or 3 subway line to 34th street from my current location, 86th street (reinforcement of information needed to get to my destination). Thus, when discussing pivotal responses and motivation, our job may be made much more difficult if we do not address and understand motivation to teach various skills, language, and communication, as well as assessing functions of behaviors.

Examples:
- scanning,
- initiations, or
- responsiveness to multiple cues.

Vignette: Pivotal Skills

Delfina was recently diagnosed with ASD and began attending a preschool disabilities class that used applied behavior analysis to teach skills. After she was assessed using the VB-MAPP, the teacher observed that her profile lacked some basic requesting skills. Seeing that Delfina often cried and grabbed to get what she wanted, the teacher decided that she would work on initiations for appropriately requesting, as well as identifying motivation for anything that Delfina might want. By targeting these pivotal skills, the teacher was ensuring that Delfina would learn to initiate appropriately based on her motivation to get her needs met. The teacher not only worked on initiations and assessing motivation at school, but went to Delfina's home and trained her parents to do the same so that skills were generalized with parents and at home.

Special Considerations

Parental involvement with pivotal skills is critical and necessary. To maximize the effectiveness of pivotal targets, it is essential that learners respond to parents and other caregivers in their environment. One must ensure that such training occurs with parents so that benefits of Pivotal Response Training (PRT) are successful and maximized. A neat aspect of PRT is that much of what is needed to implement it is found in the natural environment, and parents are taught to contingently reinforce any goal directed attempt for their child to respond. Reinforcers, motivational opportunities, and preferred activities can be observed in individuals and used immediately. There is no need to construct materials, or buy expensive toys, cards, or gadgets.

I want to teach pivotal skills because of the collateral effects these skills will have on other areas of functioning.	**Pivotal Skills** (any response that affects other behaviors in a broader and collateral way)		
Step 1: Defining your behavior is important. What does the behavior look like? (form)	*Communication initiations* are defined as the vocalization of and/or picture exchange of, sign language use of, or augmentative system use of to request, label, or converse with another person.	*Flexibility* is defined as appropriately shifting attention and/or responses to stimuli that are presented in the environment and/or by others without problematic behavior.	*Responsivity* is defined as appropriately replying verbally or physically to verbal or physical stimuli presented by others that may have multiple cues.
Step 2: What dimensions of the behavior can you measure?	Dimension 1: Can you count it as an instance of a response?	Dimension 2: Can you measure the duration of the behavior? Is it important?	Dimension 3: Can you measure when the behavior occurs in relation to other events?
Step 3: Define your behavior, write a measurable definition.	Example 1: Communication with Adrian is measured as each instance in which he independently initiates and uses the Picture Exchange Communication System (PECS) according to Phase I protocol of PECS to request tangible or edible items from another person or to stop an activity.		
	Example 2: Flexibility is defined as Adrian responding to shifts in stimuli or changes and routines in the environment without engaging in problematic behaviors such as crying, falling to the floor, or aggressions toward others.		
	Example 3: Responsivity is defined as Adrian noticing and responding to social and environmental stimuli that are presented during structured and unstructured sessions, such as looking at cards placed on a table or a saying hello to a person entering a room.		

Potential Tools
- MotivAider
- Counter
- Timer

Pivotal Behaviors References and Recommended Readings

Koegel, R. L., & Kern Koegel, L. (2006). Pivotal Response Treatment for Autism: Communication, Social and Academic Development. Brooks Publishing Company.

Skinner, B. F. (1953). Science and human behavior. New York: The Macmillan Company.

Skinner, B. F. (1957). Verbal behavior. Englewood Cliffs, NJ: Prentice Hall.

Sundberg, M. L., & Michael, J. (2001). The benefits of Skinner's analysis of verbal behavior for children with autism. *Behavior Modification, 25*(5), 698-724.

Sundberg, M. L. (2008). *Verbal Behavior Milestones Assessment and Placement Program: A language and social skills assessment program for children with autism or other developmental disabilities.* AVB Press.

SELF-HELP

Self-help skills include self-care, choice-making, and schedule-following skills. Often, we hear these described as Daily Living Skills. Many of these skills may be challenging to implement in a classroom setting because they aren't built into most curricula. However, these are the skills that are the very foundation for independent living. And while teaching these skills is often associated with the needs of individuals with disabilities, many children in the general education setting may require assistance with them as well.

Examples:

- brushing hair
- selecting food for a snack at home
- toilet training
- choosing a peer to play with
- checking a calendar
- navigating between two locations
- selecting appropriate clothing
- choosing a game to play
- setting an alarm clock
- requesting a bathroom pass
- using basic tools
- going to class when the bell rings
- cleaning dishes
- selecting items to pack for a trip
- putting batteries in a device
- putting shoes on/taking shoes off
- finding needed items in a first aid kit
- responding to a smoke alarm
- ordering food at a restaurant
- following a visual schedule
- caring for menstrual needs
- arriving to class on time
- providing medical information
- identifying allergies for a doctor

Vignette: Self-Help

Jackson is a 14-year-old student who attends a self-contained high school class for individuals with multiple disabilities. He communicates quite effectively with a software program on his iPad, has some vocal language, and is quite social in that he makes regular eye contact with others, greets individuals, and loves to please others. For leisure, he runs on the track team at school with the support of an aide who runs alongside him. He is a fast runner and enjoys the team atmosphere, in which he is very much accepted and supported because of how fast he runs. One day Jackson communicated that he needed to use the bathroom, like he ordinarily does at school. The para noticed that it had been several minutes and Jackson was not back, when he she went to check on him. She called asking if he were okay and lo and behold, Jackson vocalized, "help me, poop." He had a bowel movement for the first time at school and was unable to wipe himself. It was immediately apparent to the teaching staff that Jackson had never learned to wipe independently. When his parents were called, they informed the teacher that he usually doesn't go at school and they usually help him with the process. Needless to say, this became an immediate goal for Jackson, who otherwise was having a great adjustment to high school, but needed to work on self-care skills to increase his quality of life.

Special Considerations

In the above example, targeting such an infrequently occurring behavior in the school environment is difficult, and a consideration to target the behavior in all settings must be made so that Jackson learns the skill at each opportunity. Other considerations include:

- generalization to other environments;
- how requests should look in the natural environment; and
- setting a standard measurement may be difficult. For instance, how will you measure appropriate tooth-brushing?

Self-Help Skills

(skills that increase independence and care of self)

I want to teach self-help because of the independence my learner will gain in life.

Step 1: Defining your behavior is important. What does the behavior look like (form)?	*Self-Care* is defined as any behavior that promotes the independent care of oneself.	*Choice-Making* is defined as a selection between two or more options or choices provided visually, textually, and/or via spoken words.	*Schedule-Following* is defined as observing and following the commands of a visual/textual and/or auditory schedule of one's day and/or activity to be completed in the near or immediate future.
Step 2: What dimensions of the behavior can you measure?	Dimension 1: Can you count it as an instance of a response?	Dimension 2: Can you measure the duration of the behavior? Is it important?	Dimension 3: Can you measure when the behavior occurs in relation to other events?
Step 3: Write your definition.	Example 1: Self-Care (Toileting): Jackson will independently use the bathroom at school to wipe himself clean, after having a bowel movement. Wiping clean is defined as using toilet paper and/or toilet wet wipes to clean self until no marks remain on toilet paper/wet wipe.		
	Example 2: Choice-Making: During recess, Maria will be provided with three choices. She can go to the slide, swing, or draw with chalk on the asphalt. She will independently select one of these options, then carry through with her selection (i.e., walk to the slide or pick up the chalk).		
	Example 3: Schedule-Following: Ashton will independently follow a visual schedule to complete activities during free time. These activities will include completing puzzles, drawing, and obtaining a snack.		

Potential Tools

- Data Sheets
- Timers
- MotivAiders
- VibraLite

Self-Help: References and Recommended Readings

Azrin, N., & Foxx, R. M. (1989). *Toilet training in less than a day.* Simon and Schuster.

Cocchiola Jr., M. A., Martino, G. M., Dwyer, L. J., & Demezzo, K. (2012). Toilet training children with autism and developmental delays: an effective program for school settings. *Behavior Analysis in Practice, 5*(2), 60.

MacDuff, G. S., Krantz, P. J., & McClannahan, L. E. (1993). Teaching children with autism to use photographic activity schedules: maintenance and generalization of complex response chains. *Journal of Applied Behavior Analysis, 26*(1), 89-97.

Self-Help: References and Recommended Readings (cont'd)

Page, T. J., Iwata, B. A., & Neef, N. A. (1976). Teaching pedestrian skills to retarded persons: Generalization from the classroom to the natural environment. *Journal of Applied Behavior Analysis, 9*(4), 433-444.

Partington, J. W., & Mueller, M. M. (2012). *The Assessment of Functional Living Skills™: Basic Living Skills Assessment Protocol: An Assessment, Skills Tracking System, and Curriculum Guide for Skills that are Essential for Independence.***

Swain, J. J., Allard, G. B., & Holborn, S. W. (1982). The good toothbrushing game: a school-based dental hygiene program for increasing the toothbrushing effectiveness of children. *Journal of Applied Behavior Analysis, 15*(1), 171.

Sundberg, M. L. (2008). *VB-MAPP Verbal Behavior Milestones Assessment and Placement Program: a language and social skills assessment program for children with autism or other developmental disabilities: guide. AVB Press.****

***The Assessment of Functional Living Skills (Partington & Mueller, 2012) provides a comprehensive evaluation of self-help skills across the lifespan. It is a useful tool for assessing and measuring progress in these skill areas.*

****For younger students, AVBPress.com contains a section of Self-Care assessment questions that can be used to assess dressing, bathing and grooming, feeding and toileting as part of the electronic version of the VBMAPP tracking sheets (Sundberg, 2008). You can download the Self-Care Checklist at http://avbpress.com/updates-and-downloads.html .*

LEISURE

Helping students develop leisure skills is incredibly important. Early on in our field, practitioners were working to develop leisure skills in individuals with developmental disabilities. The leisure activities included playing darts (Schleien, Wehman, & Kiernan, 1981), learning how to dance (Lagomarcino, Reid, Ivancic, & Faw, 1984), playing video games such as Guitar Hero II™ (Blum-Dimaya, Reeve, Reeve, & Hoch, 2010), and even training to pass a soccer ball (Luyben, Funk, Morgan, Clark, & Delulio, 1986). Adding these simple skills to a learner's repertoire allows for increased opportunities for social interaction with appropriate-age peers, provides active options for leisure time, and increases a learner's independence across multiple domains. The technology of picture activity schedules has often been used to teach various leisure skills to individuals with developmental disabilities (MacDuff, Krantz, & McClannahan, 1993).

Examples:

- kicking a ball
- painting
- playing a board game
- putting together a puzzle
- reading a book independently
- playing a musical instrument
- shooting a basketball
- writing or journaling
- drawing
- playing a computer game
- riding a bike
- baking with a family member or friend

Vignette: Leisure Skills

Mrs. Clayton teaches in a classroom with twelve 7- to 8-year-old students with various developmental disabilities. On days when it is raining, Mrs. Clayton's students stay in her classroom during recess. She notices one day that three of her students do not engage in activities during recess unless directly told to do so by an adult. While the other students are playing or interacting with one another, these three students are often on their own without an activity. She decides she needs to teach them some leisure activities to keep them learning and engaged during breaks and recess, to increase the opportunities for social interaction, and to provide some relief for the adults who are constantly prompting them.

Mrs. Clayton begins training with one student, Isa, a 7-year-old boy diagnosed with ASD, on how to follow a leisure picture activity schedule. She realizes that he actually knows how to play with several toys, including putting together puzzles containing up to 24 pieces and playing a memory game, but he will not independently engage in these activities.

Through the use of a leisure picture activity schedule, Isa was taught to engage in six leisure activities: a dinosaur puzzle, playing a memory matching game with a peer, tangram pattern blocks, dot-to-dot tracing, an animal sorting game, and an app with an animal-sound matching game on the iPad. Once Isa was taught to sequentially follow his leisure activity schedule, he was able to engage in the above activities independently for a minimum of 15 minutes. In addition, the embedding of an activity (memory game) with a peer ensured that age-appropriate interactions and socialization were reinforced.

Special Considerations

- Decrease prompt dependence: student needs to be able to initiate leisure activities
- Choose age-appropriate activities and self-monitoring activities
- Pair with reinforcement so the leisure activity is actually reinforcing, and not just something we think might be reinforcing
- Ensure that leisure activities also target social interactions with others

Leisure Behavior

(skills that are free from work demands or other duties and are utilized for preferred, desirable, or reinforcing activities during free time)

I want to teach leisure behavior/skills because of the enjoyable, appropriate, adaptive use of time my learner can choose.			
Step 1: Defining your behavior is important. What does the behavior look like (form)?	*Self-Management* is defined as the personal application of behavior-change tactics that produces a desired change in behavior.		*Self-Monitoring* is defined as a procedure whereby a person systematically observes his behavior and records the occurrence or nonoccurrence of a behavior.
Step 2: What dimensions of the behavior can you measure?	Dimension 1: Can you count it as an instance of a response?	Dimension 2: Can you measure the duration of the behavior? Is it important?	Dimension 3: Can you measure when the behavior occurs in relation to other events?
Step 3: Write your definition.	Example 1: Self-Management: When recess time is indicated on a visual schedule, Isa will independently retrieve and follow the activities on his leisure picture activity schedule, rewarding his own completion of the schedule at the end of the last activity.		
	Example 2: Self-Monitoring: After each activity is completed on his leisure picture activity schedule, Isa will provide himself a token for each activity until all are completed.		

Potential Tools

- MotivAider
- Data sheets
- Token systems
- Timers
- VibraLite

Leisure: References and Recommended Readings

Blum-Dimaya, A., Reeve, S. A., Reeve, K. F., & Hoch, H. (2010). Teaching children with autism to play a video game using activity schedules and game-embedded simultaneous video modeling. *Education and Treatment of Children, 33*(3), 351-370.

Carlile, K. A., Reeve, S. A., Reeve, K. F., & DeBar, R. M. (2013). Using activity schedules on the iPod touch to teach leisure skills to children with autism. *Education and Treatment of Children, 36*(2), 33-57.

Hoch, H., McComas, J. J., Johnson, L., Faranda, N., & Guenther, S. L. (2002). The effects of magnitude and quality of reinforcement on choice responding during play activities. *Journal of Applied Behavior Analysis, 35*(2), 171-181.

Lagomarcino, A., Reid, D. H., Ivancic, M. T., & Faw, G. D. (1984). Leisure-dance instruction for severely and profoundly retarded persons: Teaching an intermediate community-living skill. *Journal of Applied Behavior Analysis, 17*(1), 71-84.

Luyben, P. D., Funk, D. M., Morgan, J. K., Clark, K. A., & Delulio, D. W. (1986). Team Sports for the severely retarded: Training a side-of-the-foot soccer pass using a maximum-to-minimum prompt reduction strategy. *Journal of Applied Behavior Analysis, 19*(4), 431-436.

MacDuff, G. S., Krantz, P. J., & McClannahan, L. E. (1993). Teaching children with autism to use photographic activity schedules: Maintenance and generalization of complex response chains. *Journal of Applied Behavior Analysis, 26*(1), 89-97.

Schleien, S. J., Wehman, P., & Kiernan, J. (1981). Teaching leisure skills to severely handicapped adults: An age-appropriate darts game. *Journal of Applied Behavior Analysis, 14*(4), 513-519.

CHANGING YOUR OWN BEHAVIOR

Often in the course of focusing on student achievement, it can be difficult to address our own behaviors within the classroom. Simultaneously, addressing your own behavior may actually be the best place to start.

It cannot be denied that many students may come in after having a bad morning at home, or may bring problems from home into the classroom. Ultimately, though, the classroom is your environment, and you have the ability to change many variables to improve your students' educational and emotional responses.

One suggestion we often make to teachers is to record themselves teaching so they can observe in a more detailed way how their behaviors are impacting the classroom (you may need to check with policies for videotaping in your school or teaching environment). You may notice that there are minor changes you can make in terms of where you stand, how you provide prompts, or how often you provide positive feedback that could have big effects on your classroom.

There's a large body of research addressing the impact of teacher behavior on student outcomes. In this section, we'll discuss a few teacher behaviors, and you may find it's beneficial for you to target one behavior for yourself.

List of behaviors that fall in this category:

- Attending to appropriate student behavior
- Providing more feedback to students
- Implementing academic tasks that decrease problem behaviors
- Changing the physical environment
- Ignoring mild inappropriate behavior/comments (not responding verbally)
- Maintaining a fast pace of instruction

Vignette: Assessing Teacher Behavior

Ms. Armstrong is an eleventh-grade classroom teacher working with students with autism. She wants to focus on providing more verbal praise during the school day. She decides to wear a MotivAider that is set to vibrate every five minutes. When she feels the vibration, she surveys the classroom and says something such as "I like how Jacob is sitting so nicely," or "Thank you for raising your hand, Saquan."

Special Considerations

It may be beneficial to have a peer or supervisor come in and suggest possible targets for behavior change for you. This can help you with goal setting and creating effective plans for behavior change.

Potential Tools

- MotivAider
- Environmental changes (moving desks)

Changing Your Own Behavior: References and Recommended Readings

Allday, R. A., Bush, M., Ticknor, N., & Walker, L. (2011). Using teacher greetings to increase speed to task engagement. *Journal of Applied Behavior Analysis, 44*(2), 393-396.

Austin, J. L., & Soeda, J. M. (2008). Fixed-time teacher attention to decrease off-task behaviors of typically developing third graders. *Journal of Applied Behavior Analysis, 41*(2), 279-283.

Bicard, D. F., Ervin, A., Bicard, S. C., & Baylot-Casey, L. (2012). Differential effects of seating arrangements on disruptive behavior of fifth grade students during independent seatwork. *Journal of Applied Behavior Analysis, 45*(2), 407-411.

Munro, D. W., Stephenson, J., & Roane, H. (2009). The effects of response cards on student and teacher behavior during vocabulary instruction. *Journal of Applied Behavior Analysis, 42*(4), 795-800.

Plavnick, J. B., Ferreri, S. J., & Maupin, A. N. (2010). The effects of self-monitoring on the procedural integrity of a behavioral intervention for young children with developmental disabilities. *Journal of Applied Behavior Analysis, 43*(2), 315-320.

Van Houten, R., & Sullivan, K. (1975). Effects of an audio cueing system on the rate of teacher praise. *Journal of Applied Behavior Analysis, 8*(2), 197.

CHANGING YOUR BEHAVIOR

Changing Your Behavior

(addressing your own behaviors that may impact student behavior, student performance, or opportunities for students to contact reinforcement)

What am I doing and saying to promote and maintain adaptive behavior and decrease problematic behavior when interacting with my student(s)?	Awareness: Reflecting on your own behaviors and considering possible changes that can be made.	Observation: Requesting observation from peers or supervisors to identify possible areas for behavior change.	
How can I take data on myself? How punishing are my actions or my words? How reinforcing are my actions or my words?	What am I doing? What would I like to change about what I do? How would I define my target behavior?	What am I saying? What would I like to change about what I do? How would I define my target verbal behavior?	
Step 1: Defining your behavior is important. What does the behavior look like (form)?	What is the topography of my behavior?	What are the contingencies maintaining my behavior?	
Step 2: What dimensions of the behavior can you measure?	Dimension 1: Can you count it as an instance of a response?	Dimension 2: Can you measure the duration of the behavior?	Dimension 3: Can you measure when the behavior occurs in relation to other events?
Step 3: Write your definition.	Example 1: (What Lisa says) Lisa recognizes that she is telling students to stop inappropriate behavior (nagging) or providing reprimands, but inappropriate student behavior is not decreasing. She defines her target behavior as: Providing positive feedback statements to students, such as "I like how you're writing neatly" or "Thank you for raising your hand." She decides to count the number of positive verbal statements she provides to students throughout instructional time after lunch (when those behaviors increase) by putting tally marks on a piece of masking tape she has attached to her clipboard.		
	Example 2: (What Lisa does) Lisa begins paying attention to her voice volume and tone. She notices she gets loud when asking students to stop a behavior. She decides to track her volume so that she can decrease loudness. She defines loud as anything over 70 decibels. She tracks this by using a volume meter on her phone during group instruction.		

CLASSWIDE BEHAVIOR CHANGE

Teachers often want to focus on improving the behavior of the entire class, rather than focusing on the behavior of only one individual. Sometimes such a task can seem daunting in that it requires behavior change of many students, but there are many evidence-based strategies you can use to address the behavior of the entire class. And there are many tools to help you measure that behavior.

In creating classwide behavior change, there are two common errors we see. First, (and most frequent) is unintentionally making the classroom a punitive environment. Instead of identifying the appropriate behaviors students exhibit, too much time and energy is spent focusing on the inappropriate behaviors. This can be exhausting for both the teacher and the students, creating an aversive environment for everyone. The second error we see is too many rules, or rules that are too broadly defined. Instead, there should only be a few rules (2-5, depending on your setting) that are clearly defined. Students should have a clear understanding of what behaviors are expected.

Examples:

- raising hands,
- remaining in seats,
- being helpful,
- being friendly/complimentary,
- lining up quickly and safely,
- sitting appropriately at circle time, and
- handing in homework efficiently.

Vignette: Classwide Behavior Change

Shane, Mario, and Orlando are in a classroom that focuses on behavioral difficulties. It is common that one student will act up by calling out or running around the classroom, and all of a sudden all three will join in on the same behaviors. When playing on the carpet, Mario will grab Legos from his peer, Shane, and often this erupts into full meltdowns for Shane. Legos are thrown, screaming and crying begin, and instructional time goes by the wayside as teachers and aides are busy trying to help each student get back on track with behaviors. When transitioning, often each student wants to be first on line or first to reach a destination. Sometimes, they refuse to get on line or leave the class because they state that they don't want to go to music, or gym, or other special classes. Moving from point A to point B becomes a behavioral episode, and once again, instructional time and learning is compromised.

To address these multiple concerns, a classwide management system was created for Mr. Caulfield's classroom. Based on research on how to implement classwide contingencies, he decided to use a traffic-light system that is leveled and focuses on promoting positive behavior. The traffic-light system runs on the idea that all students start out with "green," meaning they are engaging in the behaviors that are appropriate and are the rules of the class. Privileges are exchanged when you remain on green during check-in times. If infractions occur, the student is simply moved to the next level: yellow or red. Mr. Caulfield used transitions (moving from point A to B), raising your hand during small group instruction, and friendliness toward a peer as target behaviors to be rewarded. All of these target behaviors were role-played and taught in advance, and students were introduced to the traffic light system and what each light color meant. Once teaching of the system was completed, the staff focused on reinforcing the appropriate target behaviors.

We recommend focusing on positive behavior when such systems are used. To do that, one must develop and practice use of positive vocabulary when using such classwide behavior change systems. One example is the use of the word "reminder" instead of "warning" (especially with younger students). Because we are focusing on positive behavior, "reminder" is a more neutral way of letting a student know that they need to attend to their behavior to stay on green. If you were to issue a "warning," it has a much more negative connotation, which may be associated with punishment and can spiral into a whole host of negative interactions.

Special Considerations

Classroom management can be tough and may seem overwhelming, especially if more than one individual is engaging in problematic behavior. Focusing on one to three global behaviors for all students is highly recommended. Often, educators become concerned about the time taken away from actual instruction and may lose sight of classroom management. In our experience, focusing on behaviors first and ensuring that systems are in place to reinforce appropriate skills becomes a priority, as students need to be available to learn before instruction can take place.

I want to teach group behavior to maximize instructional time and increase prosocial behaviors.	Classwide Behavior Change		
Step 1: Define group behaviors you want to increase in your classroom.	Recruiting Attention	Efficient Transitions	Prosocial Behaviors (friendly/helpful behaviors)
Step 2: What dimension of behavior can you measure	Can you count it?	Can you measure duration of transition?	Can you count instances of defined target behaviors?
Step 3: What are your definitions?	Recruiting Attention: Student will raise hand to ask questions during small group instruction. Efficient Transitions: Student will go from point A to point B when asked. Prosocial Behaviors: Student will offer assistance to another peer when help is requested. Students will notice/recognize peer for friendly behavior and give a compliment.		

Potential Tools

- MotivAider
- Data sheets
- Timer

Classwide Behavior Change: References and Recommended Readings

Harris, V. W., & Sherman, J. A. (1973). Use and analysis of the "Good Behavior Game" to reduce disruptive classroom behavior. *Journal of Applied Behavior Analysis, 6*(3), 405-417.

Strain, P. S., & Schwartz, I. (2001). ABA and the development of meaningful social relations for young children with autism. *Focus on Autism and Other Developmental Disabilities, 16*(2), 120-128.

Tingstrom, D. H., Sterling-Turner, H. E., & Wilczynski, S. M. (2006). The good behavior game: 1969-2002. *Behavior Modification, 30*(2), 225-253.

Weeden, M., Wills, H. P., Kottwitz, E., & Kamps, D. (2016). The Effects of a Classwide Behavior Intervention for Students with Emotional and Behavioral Disorders. *Behavioral Disorders, 42*(1), 285-293.

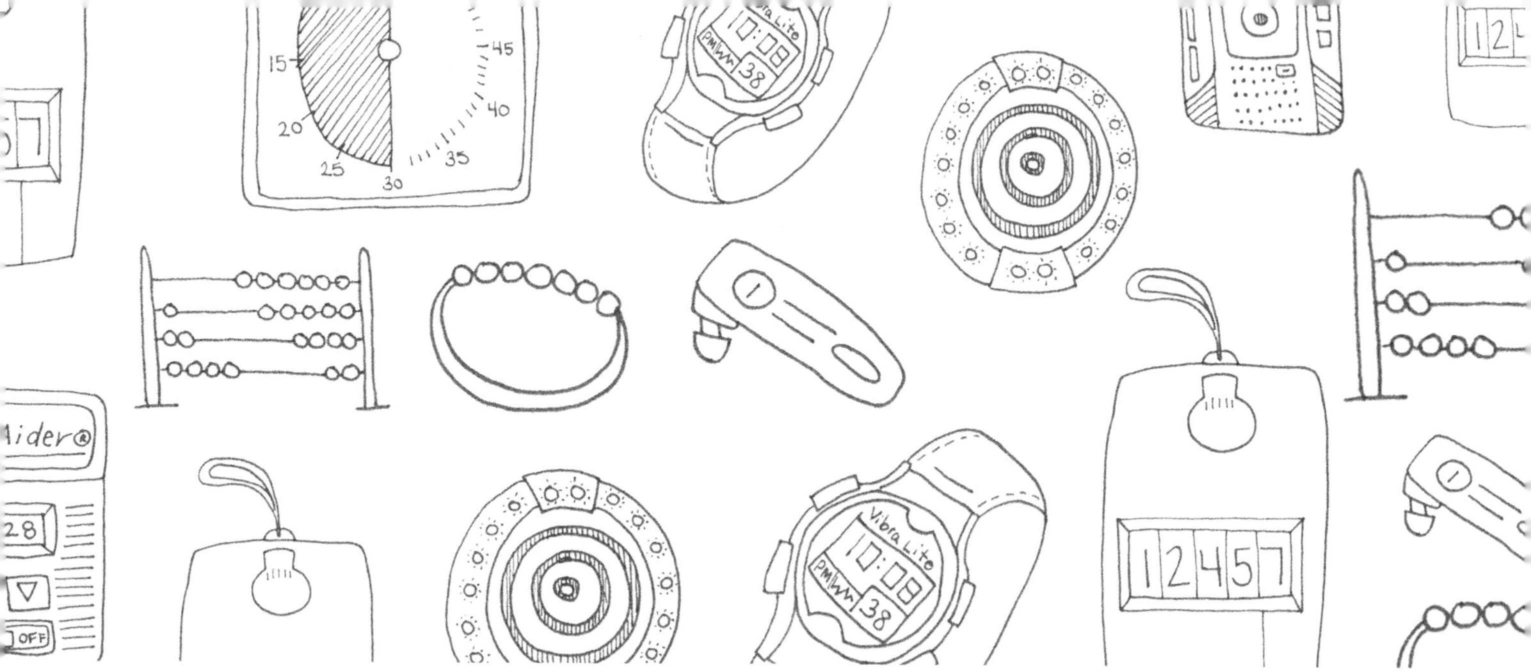

SECTION 5:
Supervisor Materials

SUPERVISION

This section of the book is devoted to supervisors of students pursuing their BCBA or BCaBA. The supervision process is a rigorous one that requires frequent observation and evaluation of the supervisee. However, it sometimes proves difficult to teach and assess new skills of the supervisee, especially when attempting to provide evidence that the supervisee is capable of applying the concepts they've learned in their work environment.

Here, we provide learning objectives, activities for teaching and use of the tools featured in previous chapters, and scenarios for practice. A rubric for each learning objective is included to assist with evaluation of the supervisee. The goal here is to bridge the gap between concept and practice, allowing for clear and objective guidelines for teaching and assessing. Each learning objective is cross-referenced with the BCBA/BCaBA Task List (5th edition).

In Applied Behavior Analysis, there are seven dimensions we consider to be essential characteristics of any intervention (Baer, Wolf, & Risley, 1968). One of these is that the intervention be technological. This means that all components of the intervention are fully identified and described well enough that anyone can replicate them. "The best rule of thumb for evaluating a procedure description as 'technological' is probably to ask whether a typically trained reader could replicate that procedure well enough to produce the same results, given only a reading of the description" (Baer, Wolf, & Risley, 1968).

Clearly defining tools and how they're used falls under the technological dimension, and it extends beyond research articles. Behavior intervention plans should also be technological so that all people implementing the intervention clearly understand it.

Pre-Data Collection Phase: Lesson One

Step ONE: Gather information from parents and professionals regarding the individual and target behavior(s).

Step TWO: Gather information on what has already been tried for interventions, types of reinforcement that have been used, and how long such interventions have been tried.

Learning Objectives: The supervisee will interview significant others to gather information on the form of the behavior, the conditions under which the behavior has typically been observed to occur, as well as variables or stimuli in the environment that can make the behavior stop. Review files and reports on individual in order to ascertain treatment history as well as behavior history.

BCBA/BCaBA Task List (5th ed.): C2, E2, E3, F1, F7

Activities For Teaching the Objectives

1. **Role Play.** Discuss the difference between direct and indirect interviews. Have the supervisee conduct one of each, with the supervisor playing the role of a parent or teacher being interviewed. Have the supervisee use the Functional Assessment Interview (FAI) by O'Neill et al. (1997) or other structured interview.

2. **Provide Clear Instructions.** You have decided to send a parent or teacher a Functional Assessment Screening Tool or FAST (2013). The supervisee should either write out or say aloud the instructions they would provide, to ensure that it was completed correctly.

3. **Engage in Descriptive Assessment Process.** This could include activities such as collecting ABC data or writing a narrative of what happened.

4. **Video + Role Play.** Watch a video of a child engaging in problematic behavior. The supervisee should identify which questions should be asked about previous interventions in order to make a more appropriate intervention. Then the supervisor should play the role of a parent or teacher, and the supervisee should interview them about previous interventions.

5. **Practice.** Select one student and conduct an interview after doing a role play. Take notes and bring them to the next supervision session. Discuss what you learned, how it might impact a behavior intervention plan, and what you might do differently in the future.

Tools to Use

You can select any tool for this objective. Part of your supervision session may be devoted to constructing your data sheet for efficiency and clarity of use to track the target behavior. You can also complete this learning objective more than once with different tools.

Scenarios for Practice

Scenario One: Darnell is a BCBA who is gathering information about a high school student with autism. Darnell speaks to the boy's mother and teacher. The mother reports that her son's problem behaviors are not occurring at home, but the teacher assures Darnell that the problem behaviors are occurring in every environment. What might Darnell do to address this issue?

Scenario Two: Carmen sends a FAST to a parent. When the FAST is returned, Carmen discovers that the parent has filled it out incorrectly, circling several responses for each item on the assessment. What should Carmen do next? Should she approach the parent to complete the FAST a second time, or select a new method for gathering information?

Rubric Pre-Data Collection Phase

	Satisfactory	Needs Improvement	Unsatisfactory
Step One: Gather information from parents and professionals regarding the individual and target behavior(s).	Interviews/talks to relevant stakeholders who know the student well to obtain information regarding behavior occurrence.	Interviews one person only, or only persons who know the student minimally.	Does not interview significant others.
Step Two: Gather information on what has already been tried for interventions, types of reinforcement that have been used, and how long such interventions have been tried.	Obtains information about: • Reinforcers, preferences, and sources of motivation. • Interventions that have already been tried, along with length and results of such interventions.	Obtains only one piece of information (e.g., reinforcers but no previous intervention history).	Does not gather information on previous interventions, reinforcers, or sources of motivation.

Pre-Data Collection Phase: Lesson Two

Step THREE: What does the behavior look like? Have you defined it? Is it measurable?

Learning Objective: Develop an operational definition.

BCBA/BCaBA Task List (5th ed.): B1, C1

Activities For Teaching the Objective

1. **Use Videos.** Select 4 behaviors to observe using YouTube videos on classes of problem behavior:
   - Disruptions (physical or vocal)
   - Aggression (mild to moderate)
   - Self-injury
   - Stereotypy

   Construct definitions based on viewing videos, taking ABC data, and writing a narrative of the behavior.

   Have a neutral person read definition and enact behavior and/or fill out data sheet after viewing video of problem behavior.

2. **Practice Writing Definitions.** The supervisee is given a list of behaviors that are not well-defined (such as "student tantrums for long periods" or "disruptive during math." The supervisee should rewrite each definition so that it is operationally defined and measureable.

3. **Observe a Behavior in the Classroom or Clinical Setting.** Observe a behavior in the supervisee's setting and create two different definitions for the behavior. For instance, in one definition the behavior may include cursing with a measure of duration, while in another cursing will include a measure of frequency. Discuss the pros and cons of each definition.

Tools to Use

Any of the tools discussed here may be appropriate for testing out an operational definition. The choice of tool would depend upon the dimension of the behavior being measured.

Scenarios for Practice

Scenario One: Alexa has defined a problem behavior exhibited by her student Annie as "speaking loudly to peers during math class." When she attempts to implement a behavior intervention, she realizes that her co-teacher has a different interpretation of "speaking loudly" than she does. How can Alexa rewrite the definition so it is clearly observable and measureable?

Scenario Two: Lena has created an operational definition for the behavior of one student in the classroom where she is consulting as a BCBA. The staff in that classroom have never received training on operational definitions for behaviors. What would you say to them to explain the importance of operational definitions? What terms would you need to introduce and define? What might you do to help them practice using such definitions?

Rubric Pre-Data Collection Phase

	Satisfactory	Needs Improvement	Unsatisfactory
Step Three: What does the behavior look like? Have you defined it? Is it measurable?	1. Operationalizes target behavior(s) in measurable and observable terms. 2. Able to identify (when relevant) early precursor behavior to target behavior. 3. Specifies unit of measurement (duration, latency, frequency/rate, intensity). 4. Specifies measurement procedures (continuous/discontinuous, time-sampling procedure, frequency of data collection, who collects data, and where).	1. Behavior definition lacks measurable criteria. 2. Specifies unit of measurement. 3. Includes vague reference to measurement procedures.	1. Behavior is inferred, lacks objectivity, and is not clearly observable. 2. Frequency of measurement is not indicated.

Pre-Data Collection Phase: Lesson Three

Step FOUR: Select appropriate tools for intervention and measurement.

Learning Objectives:

- The supervisee will demonstrate mastery of a minimum of 5 tools for intervention and measurement.
- The supervisee will identify pros and cons of a minimum of 5 tools for intervention and measurement.

BCBA/BCaBA Task List (5th ed.): C3, C4, C5, C9

Activities for Teaching the Objectives

1. **Role Play.** The supervisee will select one tool for intervention and measurement. The supervisor will act as a naive observer and the supervisee will teach the supervisor how to use the tool.
2. **Video Review.** The supervisee will select one tool for measurement. They will watch a video showing a problem behavior, operationally define that behavior, then use the tool to measure the behavior in the video.
3. **Video Model.** The supervisee will create a brief video model showing how to use a tool for intervention or measurement. The video should include steps for using the tool effectively, a demonstration of using the tool in situ, and a brief discussion of the pros and cons of using the tool.

Tools to Use

Any tools listed starting on page 13.

It's ideal to practice using many of the tools discussed in Section One so that supervisees are capable of selecting appropriate tools from a broad range of options.

Scenarios for Practice

Scenario One: Heidi is a high-school teacher. She wants to measure the number of prompts required before Anthony starts completing his class assignment. Help Heidi provide an operational definition of the behavior and the measurable dimension of the behavior, then identify a tool that will allow her to measure the behavior within her class environment.

Scenario Two: Lorena is a BCBA who has been brought in to help improve the independent living skills of Gerald, a 16-year-old boy with Down syndrome. The first task they want to teach Gerald is how to complete laundry independently. Lorena creates a task analysis detailing each step for completing laundry. While Gerald can complete each step in the task analysis, he is often very slow with completing steps, and takes a long time to start the next step after one has been completed. What type of tools might Lorena introduce to address these two issues?

	Rubric Pre-Data Collection Phase		
	Satisfactory	Needs Improvement	Unsatisfactory
Step Four: Select appropriate measurement tools for intervention and measurement.	Identifies appropriate data collection tool for target behavior and demonstrates use of tool.	Tool(s) are identified.	Tool(s) are incorrect/not identified.

Pre-Data Collection Phase: Lesson Four

Step FIVE: Create data sheet.

Learning Objectives:
- The supervisee will consider the operational definition of the behavior, the dimension of the behavior being measured, the goal for behavior change, and the environment in selecting or creating a data sheet.
- The supervisee will create a minimum of two different data sheets that include all required elements for a target behavior they have selected.

BCBA/BCaBA Task List (5th ed.): C1, C3, C4, C5, C9

Activities for Teaching Objectives

1. **Analyze a Data Sheet.** The supervisor will provide 2-3 data sheets for the supervisee to review. The supervisee will identify the key components of the data sheet and identify pros and cons of using that data sheet in their work setting.
2. **Create a Data Sheet.** The superviser will select one of the target behaviors previously discussed in a supervision session. Then the supervisee will create a data sheet for measuring behavior that would best fit their work setting.

Tools to Use

A data sheet is a tool. This idea should be explained to the supervisee so that they begin to think of ways to create sheets for the data that needs to be collected that are efficient and meet the needs of staff and students. Sometimes, variables as simple as boxes to record data can make the difference on whether or not a data point is recorded. This idea should be explained to the supervisee so that their understanding of the data sheet as a valuable tool is reinforced.

Scenarios for Practice

Scenario One: Toby teaches in a second-grade classroom. She works with students in groups of 4-6 for reading instruction, and wants to take data on the rate of correct responses for each individual student. What recommendations might you make for an efficient and effective data sheet for her to use? Are there any tools she might be able to use to make data collection easier?

Scenario Two: Reuben teaches in a high-school classroom. He has a student who breaks pencils when presented with difficult math tasks. Before implementing an intervention, Reuben wants to collect data on how long the student works before she breaks a pencil. What recommendations might you make for an efficient and effective data sheet for Reuben to use? Are there any tools he might be able to use to make data collection easier?

Rubric Pre-Data Collection Phase

	Satisfactory	Needs Improvement	Unsatisfactory
Step Five: Create data sheet	Data sheet is concise, clear, and contains the following components: • definition • intervals or place to mark occurrence or nonoccurrence of behavior • data collection schedule • data collection procedure • end totals of behavior • responses • dates • places for initials of data collector • student ID, name, or initials as appropriate	Data sheet contains at least three components, including definition and procedures to record data.	Data sheet contains definition and dates.

Data Collection Phase: Lesson One

Step ONE: Trial the data collection system and tweak any changes needed for recording behavior and tools to use.

Learning Objectives:
- The supervisee will select a data collection system, then try it out for a predetermined number of sessions or duration of time.
- The supervisee will identify pros and cons of the selected data collection system, and identify 2-3 ways the system should be improved.

BCBA/BCaBA Task List (5th ed.): C10, C11

Activities for Teaching the Objectives

1. **Role Play.** Your supervisee describes the data collection system intended for addressing the target behavior. You then role-play for ten minutes, with the supervisee acting as the teacher and the supervisor acting as the classroom student engaging in the behavior being measured. After the ten minutes are complete, discuss with the teacher the success of the data collection system. The supervisee should describe the pros and cons of the data collection system, identify areas for improvement, and discuss potential changes for improving it.

2. **Video Review.** The supervisee records the session in which he/she has tried out the data collection system. The supervisor and supervisee will watch it together, identifying areas for improvement, and discuss potential changes. After reviewing the video, it may be helpful to role-play (as described in activity 1, above) that includes changes made to the data collection system.

Tools to Use

You can select any tool for this objective. Part of your supervision session may be devoted to identifying the best tool for measuring the target behavior. You can also complete this learning objective more than one time with different tools.

Scenarios for Practice

Scenario One: Joan is a teacher in a second-grade classroom. She is working to increase hand-raising behavior for one student named Bryan. She asks the teaching assistant in her classroom to tally the number of times Bryan raises his hand and the number of times he calls out the answer for each period of the school day. During the first lesson, she notices that the teaching assistant has left the tally sheet on the desk in front of the room while working with another student struggling with the assignment. Later, during math, she is sitting next to Bryan and taking the tally data while also helping him with questions. At the end of the first day, Joan sees that for some class periods, no data was taken at all.

- What were some problems Joan encountered with her data collection system?
- What were some possible confounding variables?
- What might Joan do to improve her data collection system?

Scenario Two: Sarah is a teacher in an eleventh-grade self-contained classroom for individuals with developmental delays. Her student Lisa is engaging in a wide range of aggressive behaviors. Sarah has not yet identified the function of these behaviors. She decides to collect data on the duration of each instance of aggressive behavior. She defines aggression as hitting, kicking, grabbing, scratching, throwing objects, or banging her head on objects. Sarah wears a stopwatch around her neck and plans to start it anytime she sees an aggressive behavior and stop it whenever the aggressive behaviors stop for longer than five seconds. She has a clipboard on her desk where she will record the duration of each occurrence. During the first week of data collection, Sarah forgot to stop the stopwatch three times. She decided not to record these instances at all. She stopped data collection altogether on the eighth day because Lisa grabbed the stopwatch and pulled Sarah with great force. She still has the data, but has not analyzed it and is not sure what to do next.

- What were some problems Sarah encountered with her data collection system?
- What were some possible confounding variables?
- How might Sarah have measured the aggressive behaviors in a better way for her environment?
- What might Sarah to do to improve her data collection system?

Rubric Data Collection Phase

	Satisfactory	Needs Improvement	Unsatisfactory
Step One: Trial the data collection system and tweak any changes needed for recording behavior and tools to use.	1. Supervisee trials the data collection system for a minimum of one full data recording session using the correct tools. 2. Supervisee revises data collection system (if needed) and adjusts tools needed for data collection and recording.	Supervisee may trial system, but does not adjust system based on information obtained.	Data collection system is not trialed for problem-solving and/or improvements.

Data Collection Phase: Lesson Two

Step TWO: Decide who will be trained to collect data, and train them on the actual behaviors to be observed and measured. This involves knowing what the behavior looks like and knowing where and how to write it down on the data sheet.

Step THREE: Train all parties involved in data collection on how to use the tools for collecting data. For example, when using a MotivAider, does everyone know how to set the interval, respond to the vibration, reset it if needed, change a battery, and so on.

Learning Objectives:

- The supervisee will identify who needs to be trained to collect data.
- The supervisee will train other data collectors on how to collect the data.
- The supervisee will train other data collectors on how to use the tools for collecting data.

BCBA/BCaBA Task List (5th ed.): H9

Activities for Teaching the Objectives

1. **Model.** In this activity, the supervisor will model how to train a data collection technique. The supervisee should write down observations about the modeled training. For instance, their notes by include how a task analysis of data collection was created and explained, or the vocabulary the supervisor used in explaining data-collection methods.

2. **Role Play.** The supervisee selects the person who should be trained in the data collection method. The supervisor pretends to be that person for the purpose of this role-play. The supervisee trains the supervisor on the training method. The supervisor asks questions and summarizes what they've learned, as if they were the person being trained. Afterward, the supervisor provides feedback on how the training was provided and addresses potential problems or obstacles.

Scenarios for Practice

Scenario One: Reuben wants to take interval data for his student Alan's in-seat behavior during whole-class math instruction. Reuben has one paraprofessional in his classroom to assist students who need additional help during the lesson. He wants to use a MotivAider and the data sheet on page 17.

- Who should be trained to collect the data?
- What should training involve?
- What would be your primary objectives in training?
- How would you measure mastery of those objectives?

Scenario Two: Sabrina is teaching in a class with twelve students with autism. She has one classroom paraprofessional working in her classroom. She wants to introduce a classwide token economy to help increase prosocial behaviors with all students. These behaviors included:

- Who should be trained in the behavior intervention?
- What should training involve?
- What would be your primary objectives in training?
- How would you measure mastery of those objectives?

Rubric Data Collection Phase

	Satisfactory	Needs Improvement	Unsatisfactory
Step Two: Decide who will be trained to collect data, and train them on the actual behaviors to be observed and measured. This involves knowing what the behavior looks like and knowing where and how to write it down on the data sheet.	1. Trains relevant staff on how to observe the behavior. 2. Trains staff on use of data collection sheet and where to mark behavior data on sheet.	1. Trains relevant staff on how to observe the behavior. 2. Provides data collection sheet to staff, but no direct training on how to use it.	Reviews behavior definition with staff, but no training on observation of behavior, how to record data, or when to record data.
Step Three: Train all parties involved in data collection on how to use the tools for collecting data. For example, when using a MotivAider, does everyone know how to set the interval, respond to the vibration, reset it if needed, change a battery, and so on.	Identifies appropriate data collection tool for target behavior and demonstrates use of tool.	Tool is identified.	Tool is incorrect, not identified.

Data Collection Phase: Lesson Three

Step Four: Conduct interobserver agreement or (IOA) on the data collection process.

Learning Objectives:

- The supervisee will define IOA.
- The supervisee will demonstrate how to measure IOA.
- The supervisee will implement IOA for one intervention.
- The supervisee will identify what changes may need to be made in a case of poor IOA.

BCBA/BCaBA Task List (5th ed.): C8, D2

Activities for Teaching the Objectives

1. **Practice With a Video.** Select a video from YouTube. Provide a poor definition for the behavior in the video (such as "aggression" or "noncompliance"). If your supervisee does not ask for a more observable, measurable definition, begin the video. If he/she does ask for a better definition, provide one. While watching the video, you and your supervisee both take data on the rate of the behavior. After the video is complete, calculate your IOA. Discuss what factors might have led to a poor or strong IOA. Make improvements in the definition and the type of measurement, then watch the video a second time while taking data. With better definitions and a more appropriate measure, IOA should improve. Discuss the results.

2. **Write a Plan.** The supervisee should take an intervention he/she has already written. Write into the plan how, when, and who will take IOA data. Go over the plan with the supervisee. Discuss any potential obstacles with collecting IOA data in that setting and what should be done if IOA is poor.

3. **Implement the Plan.** The supervisee should conduct IOA in their setting. At the next meeting with his/her supervisor, they should discuss problems that occurred, ways to improve implementation of IOA, and address any problems with poor IOA.

Scenarios for Practice

Scenario One: Mary is implementing an intervention to decrease calling-out behavior in the classroom. This is particularly problematic in the afternoon, immediately after lunch. She decides she first wants to determine how frequently calling-out behavior is occurring. She is going to take frequency data. She will count the number of occurrences of calling-out, and will also have her student teacher count during the same time period. The first day they collect IOA, they only agreed on 30% of the intervals. What questions should you ask to help them strengthen IOA?

Scenario Two: Carl is a behavior analyst consulting in a kindergarten classroom. One of the students has been exhibiting tantrum behavior recently, which consists of flopping to the floor, yelling, crying, and kicking his feet up and down. The teachers report that these tantrums frequently last for up to twenty minutes. Carl decides to measure the duration of each tantrum during baseline measurement. When he collects his baseline data, he finds that tantrums don't ever last more than three minutes. What could account for the difference in these reports of durations? What might Carl consider when deciding to implement a formal IOA procedure?

Rubric Data Collection Phase

	Satisfactory	Needs Improvement	Unsatisfactory
Step Four: Conduct interobserver agreement or (IOA) on the data collection process.	1. IOA is conducted for a minimum of 25% of sessions for each phase of intervention (e.g., baseline, intervention). 2. IOA is conducted when new staff are trained in data collection.	1. IOA is conducted only once for each phase of the intervention (e.g., baseline, treatment). 2. Or, IOA is conducted for only one phase of the intervention (e.g., treatment phase).	IOA is never conducted.

Data Collection Phase: Lesson Four

Step FIVE: Clearly identify the data collection schedule.

Learning Objectives:

- The supervisee will identify the number of times each day, week, or month data needs to be collected.
- The supervisee will identify obstacles to data collection and address those obstacles in the schedule.
- The supervisee will devise a system for prompting timely data collection (including the use of calendars, reminder apps, etc.).
- The supervisee will clearly define the method of data collection (rate, frequency, etc.).

BCBA/BCaBA Task List (5th ed.): C7, C8, C9

Activities for Teaching the Objectives

1. **Write a Plan.** Have the supervisee select one behavior intervention plan they have already created. For that plan, they should select how often data collection sessions will occur and how long each data collection session will be. The supervisee should clearly define when the data will be collected. In other words, identify the onset and termination of each instance of the behavior. Finally, the supervisee should identify where the data collector will be in relation to the student. For example, will they be sitting side-by-side, will the data collector be across the room, etc.?

2. **Compare and Contrast Two Forms of Data Collection.** Have the supervisee select two possible schedules of data collection. Try out both forms, then compare and contrast them. Was one easier to implement than the other? Did one produce better IOA than the other? What obstacles were presented with each? Is there a third option that might be better than the two that were practiced?

Tools to Use

Any (depends upon the format of data collection).

Scenarios for Practice

Scenario One: Lucy is a physical education teacher. In each class period, she has 25 students. She wants to collect data to determine the activities that produce the highest levels of student participation. She does not have any teaching assistants or other staff with her, so she will have to collect the data while leading activities. She carries a clipboard, so she is able to attach a data sheet to that. She attempted to take data on the duration that at least 20 students were participating in an activity, but kept forgetting to turn off the stopwatch or lost count of students, which resulted in inconclusive data. What suggestions might you make for Lucy?

Scenario Two: Linda is working on increasing social attention through vocal praise in her first-grade classroom. She decides to collect data on the number of instances that students disrupt a lesson. She will put on a MotivAider, and each time it vibrates she will provide vocal praise to one or more students in the classroom. Simultaneously, her teaching assistant will take data throughout the morning to count the number of disruptions during lessons. What are some obstacles that might arise with this format for data collection? What might you suggest as a more appropriate data collection schedule?

Rubric Data Collection Phase

	Satisfactory	Needs Improvement	Unsatisfactory
Step Five: Clearly identify the data collection schedule.	Data collection schedule is identified and training is provided on when, where, and for how long to collect data.	Data collection schedule is identified, but no training provided on specifics of when, where, and how long to collect data.	1. Data collection schedule is not identified. 2. Data collection schedules are left to randomness and feasibility.

Post-Data Collection Phase: Lesson One

Step ONE: Review your data sheet, noting tallies, marks, comments, timings, etc. If there are any questions regarding what is on the data sheet, follow up with the person who recorded the data and get clarification.

Learning Objectives:

- The supervisee will demonstrate how to review a data sheet.
- The supervisee will address errors that are found in data collection.

BCBA/BCaBA Task List (5th ed.): C10, C11

Activities for Teaching the Objectives

1. **Role Play.** For this activity, the supervisor will play the role of a teacher who has collected data and made errors on the data sheet. The supervisee will play the role of the BCBA who is identifying those errors and demonstrating for the teacher how to avoid future errors.
2. **Provide Samples of Errors.** In this activity, the supervisor will provide 2-3 samples of data sheets with errors. The supervisee should identify the errors, then discuss how such errors should be addressed.

Tools to Use

Data sheets

Scenarios for Practice

Scenario One: Chana implemented a classwide intervention in which students earned points for raising their hand to ask a question during math class. She collected data on the number of times students raised hands for a three-week period. However, on some days there is no data at all. Additionally, some days it seems students are raising hands hundreds of times, while on others only four or five times. Further, Chana did not use the data to frequently assess the efficacy of her intervention. What suggestions would you give to Chana in order to reduce errors in recording?

Scenario Two: Chana implemented a classwide intervention in which students earned points for raising their hand to ask a question during math class. She and her teaching assistant collected data on the number of times students raised hands for a three-week period. When you review the data, you notice great discrepancies in the data. Upon asking Chana and her teaching assistant about the data, you discover that Chana was counting the number of times students raised hands, while her teaching assistant was counting the number of times students called out. What suggestions would you make to revise the data sheet and ensure that such errors do not occur again?

Rubric Post-Data Collection Phase

	Satisfactory	Needs Improvement	Unsatisfactory
Step One: Review your data sheet, noting tallies, marks, comments, timings, etc. If there are any questions regarding what is on the data sheet, follow up with the person who recorded the data and get clarification.	1. Data sheet is reviewed for comments and to ensure that data has been collected. 2. Follow-up questions are conducted for any clarifications needed.	Data sheet is reviewed for comments and to ensure that data has been collected.	Data sheet is not reviewed.

Post-Data Collection Phase: Lesson Two

Step TWO: Tally, sum, or convert any information into the actual number you will enter on your graph.

Learning Objective:

- The supervisee will look at raw data from a session and convert it to a percentage or appropriate number for graphing.

BCBA/BCaBA Task List (5th ed.): C10

Activities for Teaching the Objective

1. **Convert Raw Data.** Convert the raw data into a number for graphing or enter raw data correctly into a computer program. Provide the supervisee with several examples of raw data (or have them bring in raw data from their own students) and have them demonstrate how to convert it or enter it into a computer program that converts it.

2. **Find Errors in Computations.** Provide the supervisee with several examples of raw data in which some errors have been made. The supervisee should be able to identify errors and correct them.

Tools to Use

Calculator

Scenarios for Practice

Scenario One: Carmen has been working on multiplication facts with her students. She has three weeks of raw data for her student Desiree that has not been graphed. That data is in the table below. Help her convert the data into percentages. What information is missing from this raw data that may be important?

	Raw data	% correct	Raw data	% correct	Raw data	% correct	Raw data	% correct
Week 1	22/40		17/40		15/40		20/40	
Week 2	11/40		19/40		13/40		18/40	
Week 3	20/40		14/40		13/40		20/40	

Scenario Two: Justina has collected data on the latency of responding for her student Edward. She is uncertain about what she should do with the raw data in order to graph it. What guidance would you provide for her?

Raw latency data: Timer is started upon the end of the teacher's direction "Hang up your backpack and go to your seat." Timer is stopped when Edward's backpack is hanging and he is in his seat with his legs underneath the desk.

Date	Latency
11/06	4 minutes, 13 seconds
11/08	7 minutes, 24 seconds
11/09	5 minutes, 10 seconds

Rubric Post-Data Collection Phase

	Satisfactory	Needs Improvement	Unsatisfactory
Step Two: Tally, sum, or convert any information into the actual number you will enter on your graph.	1. Demonstrates ability to accurately tally, sum, and compile raw data. 2. Prepares totals, missing data for graph entry.	Demonstrates ability to accurately tally, sum, and compile raw data.	Data is inaccurately tallied.

Post-Data Collection Phase: Lesson Three

Step THREE: Enter your raw data for graphing onto a computer or actual paper and pencil graph and construct graph.

Learning Objectives:

- The supervisee will construct a graph with the appropriate dimensions.
- The supervisee will enter raw data on graph using paper and pencil.
- The supervisee will demonstrate mastery of any apps or computer programs used in their setting for data entry and graphing.

BCBA/BCaBA Task List (5th ed.): C10, C11

Activities for Teaching the Objectives

1. **Discuss Appropriate Dimensions for a Graph.** Provide a few sets of raw data and have the supervisee demonstrate the appropriate dimensions for a graph for that particular set of data.
2. **Graph Raw Data Using Paper and Pencil.** Have the supervisee bring in raw data from work with their clients. Use paper and pencil to construct a graph.
3. **Demonstrate Data Entry on an App or Computer Program.** Many organizations use a computerized system for data collection and graphing, such as Catalyst, ABA Therapy Tracker, or Excel. If the supervisee will be using one of these systems, then one activity should be entering raw data and accessing the graphs created by the system. It may also be beneficial to introduce the supervisee to the various systems they may encounter in their work in the future.

Tools to Use

- Paper and pencil
- Catalyst, ABA Therapy Tracker, Behavior Tracker, Excel or other apps/software used in the supervisee's organization.

Scenarios for Practice

Scenario One: Return to the raw data collected by Carmen in Step Two. Graph the data using paper and pencil. Graph the data using an app or software program.

Scenario Two: Return to the raw data collected by Justina in Step Two. Graph the data using paper and pencil. Graph the data using an app or software program.

	Rubric Post-Data Collection Phase		
	Satisfactory	Needs Improvement	Unsatisfactory
Step Three: Enter your raw data for graphing onto a computer or use an actual paper and pencil graph to construct graph.	1. Raw data is accurately transferred into computer/ software program or paper and pencil graph. 2. Graph is accurately constructed. 3. Transfer is timely and according to schedule.	Raw data is accurately transferred into computer or software program.	1. Data transfer contains errors. 2. Data transfer is not timely.

Post-Data Collection Phase: Lesson Four

Step FOUR: Analyze your data.

Learning Objectives:

- The supervisee will visually inspect a graph and analyze the trend.
- The supervisee will visually inspect a graph and analyze the variability.
- The supervisee will visually inspect a graph and analyze the levels.
- The supervisee will determine whether more data is needed to make decisions for each phase (baseline, intervention).

BCBA/BCaBA Task List (5th ed.): C11

Activities for Teaching the Objectives

1. **Define Terms Related to Analyzing Data.** The supervisee should be able to clearly explain terms related to analyzing data, including trend, variability, and levels.
2. **Analyze Graphed Data.** Provide several examples of graphs for your supervisee. The supervisee should be able to identify the trend, variability, and level for each graph.

Tools to Use

- Paper and pencil
- Ruler

Scenarios for Practice

Scenario One: Return to the graph the supervisee created for Carmen in Step Three. The supervisee should identify the trend, variability, and level for that graph.

Scenario Two: Return to the graph the supervisee created for Justina in Step Three. The supervisee should identify the trend, variability, and level for that graph.

	Rubric Post-Data Collection Phase		
	Satisfactory	Needs Improvement	Unsatisfactory
Step Four: Analyze your data.	1. Data is visually inspected on a graph and analyzed for trend, variability, and level. 2. Trend lines are drawn (if necessary). 3. Determinations are made on whether or not more data is needed for decision-making.	Data is visually inspected on a graph and analyzed for only one component (e.g. level).	Data is not visually inspected on a graph. Only raw numbers are analyzed.

Post-Data Collection Phase: Lesson Five

Step FIVE: Make a data-based decision.

Learning Objectives:

- The supervisee will use visual inspection to determine if the intervention is producing significant behavior change.
- The supervisee will use visual inspection to determine if any changes need to be made to the current intervention.
- The supervisee will use visual inspection to determine if the individual is ready for the intervention to be faded.
- The supervisee should be able to identify potential causes for data that is trending in the wrong direction or data that is highly variable.

BCBA/BCaBA Task List (5th ed.): H6, H7, H8

Activities for Teaching the Objectives

1. **Interpret Graphed Data.** Provide several examples of graphs for your supervisee. The supervisee should be able to discuss the efficacy of the intervention based on the trend, variability, and level for each graph.
2. **Adjust a Behavior Intervention Plan According to the Data.** The supervisee will look at data they have collected for a behavior intervention plan and make necessary changes according to the data.

Tools to Use

- Graphs

Scenarios for Practice

Scenario One: Return to the graph the supervisee created for Carmen in Step Three. The supervisee should identify if the intervention is producing the desired changes—and if not, what recommendations Carmen should be given.

Scenario Two: Return to the graph the supervisee created for Justina in Step Three. The supervisee should identify if the intervention is producing the desired changes—and if not, what recommendations Justina should be given.

	Rubric Post-Data Collection Phase		
	Satisfactory	Needs Improvement	Unsatisfactory
Step Five: Make a data-based decision.	1. Upon reviewing trend, variability, and level in data, a decision is made on whether to change key components of an intervention or keep as-is. 2. Decisions are explained clearly based on available data.	Data is visually inspected on a graph and analyzed for only one component (e.g. level).	Data is not visually inspected on a graph. Only raw numbers are analyzed.

Post-Data Collection Phase: Lesson Six

Step SIX: Set up your clean data sheets for the next day (or data collection period) and repeat steps 1-6.

Learning Objective:

- The supervisee will prepare materials in order to decrease response effort and decrease potential errors in data collection.

BCBA/BCaBA Task List: C7, C9

Activities for Teaching the Objective

1. **Analyze the Teaching Environment.** The supervisee should be able to discuss the teaching environment and identify the best time each day to prepare materials, as well as the location where materials should be placed.
2. **Utilize a Checklist to Ensure All Materials are Prepared.** The supervisee should create a checklist of all required materials for a particular intervention and the data collection needs. The supervisee should demonstrate use of the checklist in their setting.

Tools to Use

Paper and pencil, clipboard, bins, and measurement tools used for that particular intervention.

Scenarios for Practice

Scenario One: Jim teaches in a middle-school classroom with twelve students. He has two closets in which he can store materials, one bookshelf, and two locked cabinets. In Jim's school, he has to submit any copies he wants made two days in advance of when he needs them (he cannot make copies on his own). Between classes, Jim is required to stand in the hallway to ensure safety during transitions. What are some things Jim might want to consider in terms of preparing his data sheets to be used each day?

Scenario Two: Kari works in a specialized school. She is able to work one-to-one with each of her students, and she keeps a 3-inch binder for each student. She has created data sheets for each program she is working on with her student, but sometimes she runs out, so she rips out a piece of paper from her notebook and just jots down notes about the session, then slides it into the front pocket of the binder. She intends to update the information as soon as she finds time to make new copies of the data sheets. What would you do to help Kari create a system for setting up all the data sheets in advance?

Rubric Post-Data Collection Phase

	Satisfactory	Needs Improvement	Unsatisfactory
Step Six: Set up your clean data sheets for the next day (or data collection period) and repeat steps 1-6 in post-data collection phase.	1. Data sheets are prepared and ready for the next data collection period. 2. Tools and data sheets are easily accessible to data collector.	Data sheets are prepared and ready for the next data collection period	Data sheets are not prepared, tools are not working, or are missing or unavailable.

APPENDIX A: TASK ANALYSIS OF DATA COLLECTION

Phases of Data Collection

Pre-Data Collection Phase

1. **Talk to other professionals and parents about their concerns regarding the learner.** Gather information from parents and professionals regarding the individual and target behavior(s). Gather information on what has already been tried for interventions, types of reinforcers that have been used, and how long such interventions have been tried.
2. **Operationally define your behavior and put the definition(s) on your data sheet.** Make sure that you and your team are in agreement with the definition of your behavior(s). Ensure that your definition has measureable properties of behavior.
3. **Create your data sheet.** Input your definition for the target behavior.
4. **Select appropriate tools for intervention and measurement.**

Data Collection Phase

1. **Trial the data collection system. Make any necessary changes in recording procedures or tool selection.**
2. **Decide who will be trained to collect data and train them on the actual behaviors to be observed and measured.**
3. **Train all parties involved in data collection on how to use the tools for collecting data.**
4. **Conduct IOA.**
5. **Clearly identify the data collection schedule.**

Post-Data Collection Phase

1. **Review your data sheet, noting tallies, marks, comments, timings, etc.** If there are any questions regarding what is on the data sheet, follow up with the person who recorded the data to get clarification.
2. **Tally, sum, or convert any information into the actual number you will enter on your graph.**
3. **Enter your raw data for graphing onto a computer or actual paper and pencil graph.**
4. **Analyze your data.** What are the trends? What are the levels? What is the variability?
5. **Make a data-based decision.** Is there anything you can change about your intervention based on the visual inspection of the data? Do you have enough data points to be able to make a decision yet?
6. **Set up your clean data sheets for the next day or data collection period and repeat steps 1-6.**

REFERENCES

Autism New Jersey, (2014). Elopement and Wandering: Your guide to safety resources. [Pamphlet]. Robbinsville, NJ: Autism New Jersey.

Baer, D. M., Wolf, M. M., & Risley, T. R. (1968). Some current dimensions of applied behavior analysis. *Journal of Applied Behavior Analysis, 1*(1), 91-97.

Behavior Analyst Certification Board (2014). Professional and ethical compliance code for behavior analysts. Retrieved April 7, 2016.

Blum-Dimaya, A., Reeve, S. A., Reeve, K. F., & Hoch, H. (2010). Teaching children with autism to play a video game using activity schedules and game-embedded simultaneous video modeling. *Education and Treatment of Children, 33*(3), 351-370.

Bos, K. J., Zeanah, C. H., Smyke, A. T., Fox, N. A., & Nelson, C. A. (2010). Stereotypies in children with a history of early institutional care. *Archives of Pediatrics & Adolescent Medicine, 164*(5), 406-411.

Carr E. G., & Durand, V. (1985). Reducing behavior problems through functional communication training. *Journal of Applied Behavior Analysis, 18*(2), 111-126.

Cooper, J. O., Heron, T. E., & Heward, W. L. (2007). Applied behavior analysis. Pearson: Upper Saddle River, New Jersey.

Cote, C. A., Thompson, R. H., & McKerchar, P. M. (2005). The effects of antecedent interventions and extinction on toddlers' compliance during transitions. *Journal of Applied Behavior Analysis, 38*(2): 235-238.

Cunningham, A.B, & Schreibman, L. (2008). Stereotypy and Autism: The importance of function. *Research in Autism Spectrum Disorders, 2*(3), 469-479.

Dettmer, S., Simpson, R. L., Myles, B. S., & Ganz, J. B. (2000). The use of visual supports to facilitate transitions of students with autism. *Focus on Autism and Other Developmental Disabilities, 15*(3), 163-169.

Dictionary.com. (2017) Retrieved July 10, 2017, from http://www.dictionary.com/browse/tool.

Dyer, K., Dunlap, G., & Winterling, V. (1990). Effects of choice making on the serious problem behaviors of students with severe handicaps. *Journal of Applied Behavior Analysis, 23*(4), 515-524.

Enloe, K. A., & Rapp, J. T. (2014). Effects of noncontingent social interaction on immediate and subsequent engagement in vocal and motor stereotypy in children with autism. *Behavior Modification, 38*(3), 374-391.

Fischetti, A. T., Wilder, D. A., Myers, K., Leon-Enriquez, Y., Sinn, S., & Rodriguez, R. (2012). An evaluation of evidence-based interventions to increase compliance among children with autism. *Journal of Applied Behavior Analysis, 45*(4), 859-863.

Fisher. W., & Bowen, M. (2014, July). An Empirical Model for Individualized Assessment and Treatment of Two Types of Elopement: Goal-Directed Bolting and Aimless Wandering. Paper presented at the meeting of National Autism Conference, State College/University Park, PA.

Guardino, C. A., & Fullerton, E. (2010). Changing behaviors by changing the classroom environment. *Teaching Exceptional Children, 42*(6), 8-13.

Hanley, G. P., Iwata, B. A., & McCord, B. E. (2003). Functional analysis of problem behavior: A review. *Journal of Applied Behavior Analysis, 36*(2), 147-185.

Hanley, G., Piazza, C., & Fisher, W. (1997). Noncontingent presentation of attention and alternative stimuli in the treatment of attention-maintained destructive behavior. *Journal of Applied Behavior Analysis, 30*(2): 229-237.

Individuals with Disabilities Education Act of 2004, P.L. 93-112, 20 U.S.C. para 1400 *et seq.*

Iwata, B. A., Dorsey, M. F., Slifer, K. J., Bauman, K. E., & Richman, G. S. (1982/1994). Toward a functional analysis of self-injury. *Journal of Applied Behavior Analysis, 27*, 197-209. (Reprinted from *Analysis and Intervention in Developmental Disabilities, 2*, 3-20, 1982.)

Johnston, J. M., Pennypacker, H. S., & Green, G. (2010). *Strategies and tactics of behavioral research.* Routledge.

Koegel, R. L., & Kern Koegel, L. (2006). Pivotal Response Treatment for Autism: Communication, Social and Academic Development. Brooks Publishing Company.

Krantz, P. J., & McClannahan, L. E. (1993). Teaching children with autism to initiate to peers: Effects of a script-fading procedure. *Journal of Applied Behavior Analysis, 26*(1), 121-132.

Lagomarcino, A., Reid, D. H., Ivancic, M. T., & Faw, G. D. (1984). Leisure-dance instruction for severely and profoundly retarded persons: Teaching an intermediate community-living skill. *Journal of Applied Behavior Analysis, 17*(1), 71-84.

Lang, R., Rispoli, M., Machalicek, W., White, P. J., Kang, S., Pierce, N., Mulloy, A., Fragale, T., O'Reilly, M., Sigafoos, J., & Lancioni, G. (2009). Treatment of elopement in individuals with developmental disabilities: A systematic review. *Research in Developmental Disabilities, 30*(4), 670-681.

Lang, R., Davis, T., O'Reilly, M., Machalicek, W., Rispoli, M., Sigafoos, J., Lancioni, G., & Regester, A. (2010). Functional analysis and treatment of elopement across two school settings. *Journal of Applied Behavior Analysis, 43*(1), 113-118.

LeBlanc, L. A., Raetz, P. B., Sellers, T. P., & Carr, J. E. (2016). A proposed model for selecting measurement procedures for the assessment and treatment of problem behavior. *Behavior Analysis in Practice, 9*(1), 77-83.

Lindsley, O. R. (1968). A reliable wrist counter for recording behavior rates. *Journal of Applied Behavior Analysis, 1*(1), 77-78.

Luyben, P. D., Funk, D. M., Morgan, J. K., Clark, K. A., & Delulio, D. W. (1986). Team Sports for the severely retarded: Training a side-of-the-foot soccer pass using a maximum-to-minimum prompt reduction strategy. *Journal of Applied Behavior Analysis, 19*(4), 431-436.

MacDuff, G. S., Krantz, P. J., & McClannahan, L. E. (1993). Teaching children with autism to use photographic activity schedules: Maintenance and generalization of complex response chains. *Journal of Applied Behavior Analysis, 26*(1), 89-97.

Marcus, B. A., Vollmer, T. R., Swanson, V., Roane, H. R., & Ringdahl, J. E. (2001). An experimental analysis of aggression. *Behavior Modification 25*(2), 189-213.

Mason, G. J. (2006). Deprivation stereotypies in human children: The case of the Romanian orphans. Stereotypic Behaviour in Captive Animals: Fundamentals and Applications to Welfare.

Mattos, R. L. (1968). A manual counter for recording multiple behaviors. *Journal of Applied Behavior Analysis, 1*(2), 130-130.

McClannahan, L. E., & Krantz, P. J. (2006). *Teaching conversation to children with autism: Scripts and script fading.* Bethesda, MD: Woodbine House.

Minshawi, N. R., Hurwitz, S., Fodstad, J. C., Beibl, S., Morriss, D. H., & McDougle, C. J. (2014). The association between self-injurious behaviors and autism spectrum disorders. *Psychology Research and Behavior Management, 7*, 125-136.

O'Neill, R. E., Horner, R. H., Ablin, R. W., Sprague, J. R., Storey, K., & Newton J. S. (1997). Functional assessment and program development for problem behavior: A practical handbook (2nd ed.). Pacific Grove, CA: Brooks/Cole.

Parsons, M. B., Reid, D. H., Reynolds, J., & Baumgarner, M. (1990). Effects of chosen versus assigned jobs on the work performance of persons with severe handicaps. *Journal of Applied Behavior Analysis, 23*(2), 253-258.

Parsons, M. B., & Reid, D. H. (2011). Reading groups: A practical means of enhancing professional knowledge among human service practitioners. *Behavior Analysis in Practice, 4*(2), 53-60.

Piazza, C. C., Hanley, G. P., Bowman, L. G., Ruyter, J. M., Lindauer, S. E., & Saiontz, D. M. (1997). Functional analysis and treatment of elopement. *Journal of Applied Behavior Analysis, 30*(4), 653-672.

Reimers, T. M., & Wacker, D. P. (1988). Parents' ratings of the acceptability of behavioral treatment recommendations made in an outpatient clinic: A preliminary analysis of the influence of treatment effectiveness. *Behavioral Disorders, 14*(1), 7-15.

Richling, S. M., Rapp, J. T., Carroll, R. A., Smith, J. N., Nystedt, A., & Siewert, B. (2011). Using noncontingent reinforcement to increase compliance with wearing prescription prostheses. *Journal of Applied Behavior Analysis, 44*(2), 375-379.

Sarokoff, R. A., Taylor, B.A., & Poulson, C. L. (2001). Teaching children with autism to engage in conversational exchanges: Script-fading with embedded textual stimuli. *Journal of Applied Behavior Analysis, 34*(1), 81-84.

Schleien, S. J., Wehman, P., & Kiernan, J. (1981). Teaching leisure skills to severely handicapped adults: An age-appropriate darts game. *Journal of Applied Behavior Analysis, 14*(4), 513-519.

Schulze, M. A. (2016). Self-management strategies to support students with ASD. *Teaching Exceptional Children, 48*(5), 225-231.

Skinner, B. F. (1953). Science and human behavior. New York: The Macmillan Company.

Skinner, B. F. (1957). Verbal behavior. Englewood Cliffs, NJ: Prentice Hall.

Sundberg, M. L., & Michael, J. (2001). The benefits of Skinner's analysis of verbal behavior for children with autism. *Behavior Modification, 25*(5), 698-724.

Sundberg, M. L. (2008). *VB-MAPP Verbal Behavior Milestones Assessment and Placement Program: A language and social skills assessment program for children with autism or other developmental disabilities.* AVB Press.

Tiger, J. H., Hanley, G. P., & Bruzek, J. (2008). Functional communication training: A review and practical guide. *Behavior Analysis in Practice 1*(1), 16-23.

Twardosz, S., Cataldo, M. F., & Risley, T. R. (1974). Open environment design for infant and toddler day care. *Journal of Applied Behavior Analysis, 7*(4), 529-546.

Ulke-Kurkcuoglu, B., & Kircaali-Iftar, G. (2010). A comparison of the effects of providing activity and material choice to children with autism spectrum disorders. *Journal of Applied Behavior Analysis, 43*(4), 717-721.

Waters, M. B., Lerman, D. C., & Hovanetz, A. N. (2009). Separate and combined effects of visual schedules and extinction plus differential reinforcement on problem behavior occasioned by transitions. *Journal of Applied Behavior Analysis, 42*(2), 309-313.

Wilder, D. A., Chen, L., Atwell, J., Pritchard, J., & Weinstein, P. (2006). Brief functional analysis and treatment of tantrums associated with transitions in preschool children. *Journal of Applied Behavior Analysis, 39*(1), 103-107.

Wilder, D. A., Normand, M., & Attwell, J. (2005). Noncontingent reinforcement as treatment for food refusal and associated self-injury. *Journal of Applied Behavior Analysis, 38*(4), 549-553.

Worthy, R. C. (1968). A miniature, portable timer and audible signal-generating device. *Journal of Applied Behavior Analysis, 1*(2), 159.

RECOMMENDED READINGS

Ahearn, W. H., Clark, K. M., MacDonald, R. P., & Chung, B. I. (2007). Assessing and treating vocal stereotypy in children with autism. *Journal of Applied Behavior Analysis, 40*(2), 263-275.

Ahrens, E. N., Lerman, D. C., Kodak, T., Worsdell, A. S., & Keegan, C. (2011). Further evaluation of response interruption and redirection as treatment for stereotypy. *Journal of Applied Behavior Analysis, 44*(1), 95-108.

Allday, R. A., Bush, M., Ticknor, N., & Walker, L. (2011). Using teacher greetings to increase speed to task engagement. *Journal of Applied Behavior Analysis, 44*(2), 393-396.

Anna, D., Roane, H. S., & Veenstra, R. A. (2011). Functional analysis and treatment of coprophagia. *Journal of Applied Behavior Analysis, 44*(1), 151-155.

Austin, J. L., & Soeda, J. M. (2008). Fixed-time teacher attention to decrease off-task behaviors of typically developing third graders. *Journal of Applied Behavior Analysis, 41*(2), 279-283.

Azrin, N., & Foxx, R. M. (1989). *Toilet training in less than a day.* Simon and Schuster.

Bicard, D. F., Ervin, A., Bicard, S. C., & Baylot-Casey, L. (2012). Differential effects of seating arrangements on disruptive behavior of fifth grade students during independent seatwork. *Journal of Applied Behavior Analysis, 45*(2), 407-411.

Bird, F., Dores, P. A., Moniz, D., & Robinson, J. (1989). Reducing severe aggressive and self-injurious behaviors with functional communication training. *American Journal of Mental Retardation, 94*(1), 37-48.

Bloom, S. E., Iwata, B. A., Fritz, J. N., Roscoe, E. M., & Carreau, A. B. (2011 Classroom application of a trial-based functional analysis. *Journal of Applied Behavior Analysis, 44*(1), 19-31.

Call, N. A., Pabico, R. S., Findley, A. J., & Valentino, A. L. (2011). Differential reinforcement with and without blocking as treatment for elopement. *Journal of Applied Behavior Analysis, 44*(4), 903-907.

Call, N. A., Simmons, C.A., Lomas Mevers, J. E., & Alvarez, J. P. (2015). Clinical outcomes of behavioral treatments for pica in children with developmental disabilities. *Journal of Autism and Developmental Disorders, 45*(7), 2105-2114.

Carlile, K. A., Reeve, S. A., Reeve, K. F., & DeBar, R. M. (2013). Using activity schedules on the iPod touch to teach leisure skills to children with autism. *Education and Treatment of Children, 36*(2), 33-57.

Carr, E. G., Newsom, C. D., & Binkoff, J. A. (1980). Escape as a factor in the aggressive behavior of two retarded children. *Journal of Applied Behavior Analysis, 13*(1), 101-117.

Cocchiola Jr., M. A., Martino, G. M., Dwyer, L. J., & Demezzo, K. (2012). Toilet training children with autism and developmental delays: An effective program for school settings. *Behavior Analysis in Practice, 5*(2), 60.

Dib, N., & Sturmey, P. (2007). Reducing student stereotypy by improving teachers' implementation of discrete-trial teaching. *Journal of Applied Behavior Analysis, 40*(2), 339-343.

Donaldson, J. M., & Vollmer, T. R. (2011). An evaluation and comparison of time-out procedures with and without release contingencies. *Journal of Applied Behavior Analysis, 44*(4), 693-705.

Dracobly, J. D., & Smith, R. G. (2012). Progressing from identification and functional analysis of precursor behavior to treatment of self-injurious behavior. *Journal of Applied Behavior Analysis, 45*(2), 361-374.

Falcomata, T. S., Roane, H. S., Feeney, B. J., & Stephenson, K. M. (2010). Assessment and treatment of elopement maintained by access to stereotypy. *Journal of Applied Behavior Analysis, 43*(3), 513-517.

Fisher, L., Ames, E. W., Chisholm, K., & Savoie, L. (1997). Problems reported by parents of Romanian orphans adopted to British Columbia. *International Journal of Behavioral Development, 20*(1), 67-82.

Hagopian, L. P., Fisher, W. W., Sullivan, M. T., Acquisto, J., & LeBlanc, L. A. (1998). Effectiveness of functional communication training with and without extinction and punishment: A summary of 21 inpatient cases. *Journal of Applied Behavior Analysis, 31*(2), 211-235.

Hanley, G. P. (2012). Functional assessment of problem behavior: Dispelling myths, overcoming implementation obstacles, and developing new lore. *Behavior Analysis in Practice, 5(1),* 54-72.

Harris, V. W., & Sherman, J. A. (1973). Use and analysis of the "Good Behavior Game" to reduce disruptive classroom behavior. *Journal of Applied Behavior Analysis, 6*(3), 405-417.

Hoch, H., McComas, J. J., Johnson, L., Faranda, N., & Guenther, S. L. (2002). The effects of magnitude and quality of reinforcement on choice responding during play activities. *Journal of Applied Behavior Analysis, 35*(2), 171-181.

Kennedy, C. H., & Itkonen, T. (1993). Effects of setting events on the problem behavior of students with severe disabilities. *Journal of Applied Behavior Analysis, 26*(3), 321-327.

Kennedy, C. H., Meyer, K. A., Knowles, T., & Shukla, S. (2000). Analyzing the multiple functions of stereotypical behavior for students with autism: Implications for assessment and treatment. *Journal of Applied Behavior Analysis, 33*(4), 559-571.

Kurtz, P. F., Chin, M. D., Huete, J. M., Tarbox, R. S., O'Connor, J. T., Paclawskyj, T. R., & Rush, K. S. (2003). Functional analysis and treatment of self-injurious behavior in young children: A summary of 30 cases. *Journal of Applied Behavior Analysis, 36*(2), 205-219.

Lang, R., O'Reilly, M., Sigafoos, J., Machalicek, W., Rispoli, M., Lancioni, G. E., & Fragale, C. (2010). The effects of an abolishing operation intervention component on play skills, challenging behavior, and stereotypy. *Behavior Modification, 34*(4), 267-289.

McCord, B. E., Thomson, R. J., & Iwata, B. A. (2001). Functional analysis and treatment of self-injury associated with transitions. *Journal of Applied Behavior Analysis, 34*(2), 195-210.

McCord, B. E., Grosser, J. W., Iwata, B. A., & Powers, L. A. (2005). An analysis of response blocking parameters in the prevention of pica. *Journal of Applied Behavior Analysis, 38*(3), 391-394.

MacDuff, G. S., Krantz, P. J., & McClannahan, L. E. (1993). Teaching children with autism to use photographic activity schedules: maintenance and generalization of complex response chains. *Journal of Applied Behavior Analysis, 26*(1), 89-97.

Munro, D. W., Stephenson, J., & Roane, H. (2009). The effects of response cards on student and teacher behavior during vocabulary instruction. *Journal of Applied Behavior Analysis, 42*(4), 795-800.

Murphy, H. A., Hutchison, J. M., & Bailey, J. S. (1983). Behavioral school psychology goes outdoors: The effect of organized games on playground aggression. *Journal of Applied Behavior Analysis, 16*(1), 29-35.

Page, T. J., Iwata, B. A., & Neef, N. A. (1976). Teaching pedestrian skills to retarded persons: Generalization from the classroom to the natural environment. *Journal of Applied Behavior Analysis, 9*(4), 433-444.

Partington, J. W., & Mueller, M. M. (2012). *The Assessment of Functional Living SkillsTM: Basic Living Skills Assessment Protocol: An Assessment, Skills Tracking System, and Curriculum Guide for Skills that are Essential for Independence.*

Pelios, L., Morren, J., Tesch, D., & Axelrod, S. (1999). The impact of functional analysis methodology on treatment choice for self-injurious and aggressive behavior. *Journal of Applied Behavior Analysis, 32*(2), 185-195.

Piazza, C. C., Moes, D. R., & Fisher, W. W. (1996). Differential reinforcement of alternative behavior and demand fading in the treatment of escape-maintained destructive behavior. *Journal of Applied Behavior Analysis, 29*(4), 569-572.

Plavnick, J. B., Ferreri, S. J., & Maupin, A. N. (2010). The effects of self-monitoring on the procedural integrity of a behavioral intervention for young children with developmental disabilities. *Journal of Applied Behavior Analysis, 43*(2), 315-320.

Strain, P. S., & Schwartz, I. (2001). ABA and the development of meaningful social relations for young children with autism. *Focus on Autism and Other Developmental Disabilities, 16*(2), 120-128.

Swain, J. J., Allard, G. B., & Holborn, S. W. (1982). The good toothbrushing game: a school-based dental hygiene program for increasing the toothbrushing effectiveness of children. *Journal of Applied Behavior Analysis, 15*(1), 171.

Tarbox, R. S. F., Wallace, M., & Williams, L. (2003). Assessment and Treatment of Elopement: A replication and extension. *Journal of Applied Behavior Analysis 36*(2), 239-244.

Thomas, D. R., Becker, W. C., & Armstrong, M. (1968). Production and elimination of disruptive classroom behavior by systematically varying teacher's behavior. *Journal of Applied Behavior Analysis, 1*(1), 35-45.

Thompson, R. H., Fisher, W. W., Piazza, C. C., & Kuhn, D. E. (1998). The evaluation and treatment of aggression maintained by attention and automatic reinforcement. *Journal of Applied Behavior Analysis, 31*(1), 103-116.

Tingstrom, D. H., Sterling-Turner, H. E., & Wilczynski, S. M. (2006). The good behavior game: 1969-2002. *Behavior Modification, 30*(2), 225-253.

Van Houten, R., & Sullivan, K. (1975). Effects of an audio cueing system on the rate of teacher praise. *Journal of Applied Behavior Analysis, 8*(2), 197.

Weeden, M., Wills, H. P., Kottwitz, E., & Kamps, D. (2016). The Effects of a Classwide Behavior Intervention for Students with Emotional and Behavioral Disorders. *Behavioral Disorders, 42*(1), 285-293.

Woo, C. C., & Leon, M. (2013). Environmental enrichment as an effective treatment for autism: A randomized controlled trial. *Behavioral Neuroscience, 127*(4), 487-497.

Woo, C. C., Donnelly, J. H., Steinberg-Epstein, R., & Leon, M. (2015). Environmental enrichment as a therapy for autism: A clinical trial replication and extension. *Behavioral Neuroscience, 129*(4), 412.

Worsdell, A. S., Iwata, B. A., Hanley, G. P., Thompson, R. H., & Kahng, S. W. (2000). Effects of continuous and intermittent reinforcement for problem behavior during functional communication training. *Journal of Applied Behavior Analysis 33*(2), 167-79.

Zarcone, J. R., Iwata, B. A., Vollmer, T. R., Jagtiani, S., Smith, R. G., & Mazaleski, J. L. (1993). Extinction of self-injurious escape behavior with and without instructional fading. *Journal of Applied Behavior Analysis, 26*(3), 353-360.